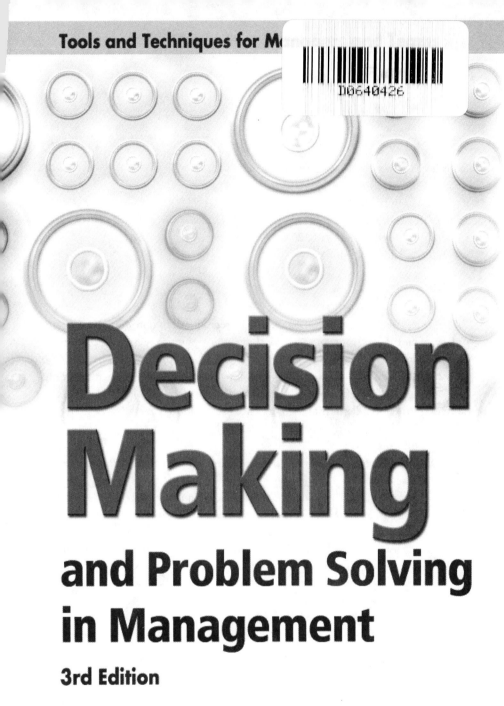

Decision Making
and Problem Solving
in Management

3rd Edition

Robert H. Vaughn

Published by Crown Custom Publishing, Inc.

Crown Custom Publishing, Inc.
1656 Pearl Road, Brunswick, Ohio 44212
(330) 273-4900 or (877) 225-8820
www.crowncustompublishing.com

Ordering Information

Individual sales: This book can be ordered direct from Crown Custom Publishing, Inc. at the address above.

Quantity sales: Special discounts are available on quantity purchases by corporations, associations, and others. For details, contact Crown Custom Publishing, Inc. at the address above.

Orders for college textbook/course adoption use: Please contact Crown Custom Publishing, Inc. at (877) 225-8820.

ISBN 978-1-933403-18-2
Printed in the United States of America

Library of Congress Cataloging-in-Publication Data
First Edition   10 9 8 7 6 5 4 3 2 1

Production Coordinator: Carl L. Wirick
Copyediting: Susan Vaughn
Design: Tia Andrako

TABLE OF CONTENTS

FORWARD!

(Technically, it should be *Foreword,* but somehow I like this better! – R.V.)

Dear Readers:

Welcome to the start of an exciting journey! A journey not in place and time, but into the complex cognitive processes of Decision Making and Problem Solving. It's an important *human* endeavor, as well as an essential *management* skill. You have already made dozens to hundreds of decisions and solved at least a few problems since you woke up this morning, so the journey is one that you've made many times. As you read this book, however, I ask that you take a fresh look, not where you arrived (the final decision or solution), but how you got there. It's fascinating. If you have never before taken something apart to see how it works, then you're in for a treat. I was sent to my room many times for such activities as a child, but I learned a lot.

Purpose of this Book

Decision making and problem solving can be quite complex processes, but using different kinds of "tools" can help a person approach them more easily and more effectively. In recent years there has been a tendency for college courses and business seminars on this subject to become over-systematized. Graduate programs in management science, especially, have espoused elaborate procedures requiring an in-depth background in statistics, as well as sophisticated models into which massive amounts of data must be entered. Management science does have its place, however most business and personal decisions simply don't require all of this.

The typical manager or entrepreneur can make nearly all the decisions and solve nearly all the problems they face by just using a few simple concepts. Seldom is it necessary to deal with primary research or economic forecasting projections. Managers may just need to do things like figure inventory requirements or staffing needs for their department, or make some other routine decisions or solve routine control problems. Sophisticated models would, for these purposes, probably get in the way and be inefficient.

This book describes and advocates a "Back to Basics" approach to decision making and problem solving which is appropriate for all but upper level managers in large organizations, and even for them at times.

However risky it is to do so, this book is designed to serve two purposes:

First, it is created as an introductory or supplemental academic text on the important subjects of Decision Making and Problem Solving in Management. The reader will gain an improved sense of the components and process of these critical parts of the job of a manager.

Second, it is a book which can be of real, practical value on the job. It is written for people who need to make business or organizational decisions and solve problems. You need not be an expert or have an MBA. Most of the tools discussed in this book require no computer or math skills above high school level. (Of course, if you happen to understand math or computers, you may be able to make even greater use of these tools.) Some of the tools you'll learn apply to any aspect of life; others only apply to certain kinds of business problems or decisions.

Keep it on your shelf at work and pull it down when you're faced with a tough problem to solve or decision to make. Remind yourself about the process, then choose an appropriate tool. Apply it according to the instructions, and you should be able to develop an answer that works. If it doesn't, try another tool until you find one that does what you need.

Topic Coverage

The book has two different types of chapters. In *Part I*, Chapters One through Seven cover the usual information content about the title subjects which would be expected in a textbook. It begins with an overview of the management process, focusing on planning and control. Then the decision making and problem solving processes are dissected into their parts and each is examined in turn. Next, the subjects of creativity and analysis are treated, followed by a discussion of other factors which influence how decisions are made and problems are solved. Finally, since most decisions and solutions result in a need to make changes of some sort, Chapter Seven provides a suggested format to propose implementation of the new way of doing things.

The four chapters in *Part II* present step by step directions for using various decision making and problem solving tools. Chapter Eight discusses common planning and control tools such as budgets, and the subsequent chapters cover various tools which can be used to improve creativity, to do a more effective analysis of options which have been developed, and to evaluate organizational productivity. All of the mathematics related to these tools is relegated to the appendix.

The Computer Support Disk

A bonus feature with the 3rd edition of this book is a computer support disk. If you've bought the book new, it should be included. Here's what you'll find on the disk:
- A brief pre- and post-test on the subject of decision making (with answers)
- A series of printable forms which can be used to structure a decision making process.
- A series of printable forms which can be used to develop a proposal.
- Templates for many of the tools described in the last four chapters.
- Answers to some of the chapter questions and exercises.
- Hyperlinks to selected relevant websites.
- And various other useful files.

The contents of the disk may change with subsequent reprints of the 3rd edition.

Acknowledgments

As a new college faculty member in the 1970's, I began teaching a course titled *Decision Making in Management* at one of the very few community colleges in the country to have such a course at the time. It was originally created by one of my early colleagues, Professor Jessie Stocking. We did not use a textbook for the course, since the texts we found were either (1) overly encumbered with statistical models and esoteric theories, or (2) case oriented without a sufficient structure to meet the needs of the hands-on supervisor or entrepreneur who typically attended the course.

Ms. Stocking created a handout package that included many of the topics which eventually found their way into this book. It was practical and had sufficient structure, but could still be tackled by the mathphobics who wanted to manage their organizations more effectively. That handout package was the precursor to this effort.

I appreciate the support of my colleagues and my wife, Susan, in the creation of this project. Thanks, also, to Roger Williams, a friend and business partner who was responsible for moving this book into a much wider market. Other help was provided by Carl Wirick, my publisher for this third edition, and Tia Andrako for the graphic design. Finally, I particularly appreciate the constructive comments from many of my former students and seminar participants over the years who have helped me define the needs of their organizations to improve decision making and problem solving.

If you have comments or questions about this book, you can contact the author through the web page at www.ArvonManagement.com.

Robert H. Vaughn, PhD
Arvon Management Services
September, 2007

PART 1

The Concepts
and Process

CHAPTER 1

The Role of
Decision Making
in Management

*I knew a businessman who had so much trouble making decisions,
that when he was asked his favorite color, he always said, "Plaid."*
– Anonymous

Chapter Objectives:

This chapter is designed to enable the reader to ....

- understand the importance of decision making and problem solving in business.
- gain an historical perspective on the study of management.
- understand why the concepts of decision making and problem solving are even more important today than in the past.

M any years ago, I was teaching part-time for a university on the Gulf Coast. I have several fond memories of the place, but one which relates to this book was an encounter with one of my students on a class break during the 12th or 13th week of the semester.

I was teaching Principles of Management, and she made the comment, "Professor Vaughn, so far you haven't taught us anything in this course that isn't common sense."

I responded, "Well, we still have a couple weeks left. I hope I can keep that record intact."

The student's point was well taken. Much of good management seems to be common sense. But common sense isn't always as "common" or obvious as it seems. Take, for example, Frederick Taylor's study of the process of shoveling coal into a blast furnace in a steel mill over a century ago.

Shoveling coal requires only common sense and the physical ability to do that type of work. Yet Taylor broke the process into minute components – the shape of the shovel, the size of the blast furnace door, the duration of rest breaks, etc. – and studied each of these to try to make it better. In six months, he'd improved the coal shoveling productivity nearly 800 percent.

What seemed to be a "common sense" operation was made easier and better through a detailed analysis of the structure and process. In fact, Alfred North Whitehead points out that common sense is a bad master. He says, "The sole criterion for judgment is that new ideas shall look like old ones."

We learn complex jobs best when we break them into pieces, learn one at a time, then put them together. Common sense alone doesn't give us the structure by which that can be done.

Managing is a complex job. We can't learn it all at once, so we have to break it down into pieces and study them in isolation.

Two of the many things managers must do are *planning* and *control*. Further breaking down those tasks into their pieces, we find they both include stages of decision making and problem solving. So, to manage anything, we have to be able to solve problems and make decisions.

This book will focus on problem solving and decision making as they relate to the management functions of planning and controlling. This is certainly not to say that other functions of management such as organizing, communicating and leading aren't important. They are. But the others: a) don't lend themselves as well to structured tools and quantitative techniques, and b) actually themselves require decision making and problem solving. (More on that later.)

Decisions Are Inevitable

Everybody makes decisions.

Of course, some decisions are more important than others. "What do I wear to-day?" and "Which house should I buy?" certainly have different significance for the average person. Most days you give only a few moments' thought to your clothing, but buying a house seems much more complex. People usually spend weeks, if not months, making this decision.

Decision making is a key element in the process of management.

The decision making *process*, however, is essentially the same for both of these decisions. And that's what you'll be learning from this book: a process through which all decisions are made and problems are solved. In business organizations, decision making is how "Management Happens."

McCall and Kaplan in their excellent book ***Whatever It Takes - The Realities of Managerial Decision Making,*** say that relatively few management decisions are made or problems solved in "straightforward" ways. Most are convoluted with much fuzziness and backtracking. No doubt that's true. But, just as letters of the alphabet are the underlying structure which you must know before you can write words and sentences, so too, knowing the steps underlying the structure of problem solving and decision making is invaluable in dealing with those processes in the real world.

Decision making is the basic foundation of the process of management. Ask a manager what she or he does, and the subject of decision making will inevitably be mentioned. But before we can begin to dissect this process, we need the larger perspective of management. We can't understand the significance of Babe Ruth or Pete Rose unless we first have some sense of what baseball and gambling are all about. (Sorry, Pete.) So our discussion begins with the historical perspective on this job called management.

What is management, and how is it done? It's a complex process. The following few pages give a very brief history of the study of management. The reader is referred to various textbooks on the subject, several of which are listed in the bibliography of this book.

A Brief History of Management

Management, according to George Labovitz, is perhaps the oldest profession in the world (regardless of what you've heard about those other professions!). He cites the opening scene from the critically acclaimed PBS series *Ascent of Man*, in which Brownowski suggests, "You can't have civilization until you have management."

At whatever point human beings attempted to do things which required two or more individuals to work together, management occurred. Someone had to plan and coordinate the efforts of the participants in order to achieve a goal. This probably means that management goes back to Adam and Eve. It was not recorded which (Adam or Eve) was the manager and which was the subordinate, but if they were the first two to work together towards a common goal, then **one** of them managed.

So, management has occurred throughout history. Strangely enough, though, management was not really studied as a separate category of work until the 20th century. It's true that it happened; we have thousands of historical examples from which we can imply the existence of management: Moses' delegation of authority, the Roman legions, the early Christian church, Hannibal crossing the Alps, and on and on.

But, so far as we know, no systematic studies on the *process* of management were done.

The fact is that few things, outside of armies and governments and a couple of religious bodies, were large and complex enough to require professional management until the industrial revolution. And even then, so much needed to be learned just to deal with the man-machine interface that great improvements in operations could be made with relatively little thought.

A brief history of management helps to understand its complexity and how decision making tools can help make managing easier.

True, Niccolo Machiavelli discussed leadership strategies in his legendary *The Prince*, written in 1614. But he really only touched on management in an abstract (and some would say cynical) way. Even the person we call the "father of scientific management," Frederick W. Taylor, focused mainly on production and industrial engineering techniques more than management in his late 19th century studies. Admittedly, Taylor did develop a number of "management" ideas in the late nineteenth and early twentieth century. Some of those ideas survived, but many no longer seem to apply. Some of his ideas were just plain wrong, though that is the case with much of science in the early development of any field. (Read "A Short History of Nearly Everything" by Bill Bryson if you think that science is really ever logically developed. The same is true for so-called management science.)

The first person to give us a structure by which we could examine the entire process of management was a Frenchman named Henri Fayol. He retired as the superintendent of a large steel producing plant in France. His writing early last century (translated into English in the 1940's) was fundamental to the understanding of how management occurs. Fayol said that managers do things which workers don't do. They plan, organize, command, coordinate and control the work of other people to insure that an organization's goals are reached.

Fayol said a lot of other things about how management was structured, and many subsequent management theorists have refined and updated his work many times and added their own concepts. But the whole complex process of management still defies a concise description.

Taylor's early success in applying the process of science to the study of management led to more schools of thought which used quantitative and economic models. One of the most significant experiments into the process of management ever done was originally undertaken to further develop Taylor's idea of "one best way" to perform manual tasks. Harvard University joined with Western Electric Company in the mid 1920's to use the Hawthorne plant of that company as an experimental base to better develop Taylor's ideas.

What came to be known as "The Hawthorne Studies" were undertaken to further quantify and structure the process of production. As they progressed, however, a number of events occurred which couldn't be explained by the quantifiable data collected. For example, worker productivity improved as lights were dimmed, then continued to improve as they were raised. Taylor's ideas of piecework as a motivator were shown to be very inconsistent, and so on. The result was an evolution of the study into the beginning of what is now called organizational behavior theory.

We learned from the Hawthorne Studies that understanding human nature and group processes can be as important – and probably more important – than developing sophisticated quantitative measures and structured techniques for performing tasks.

The lessons from the Hawthorne Studies have provided a basis for many further studies and management developments along the lines of dealing with people. Frederick Herzberg in the mid-1950's attempted to explain why some of the concepts emerging from Hawthorne didn't always work. He theorized that workers were more productive when they felt they'd been allowed to participate in the design of and decision making about their jobs. Most other well-known experts in management, including people such as Peter Drucker and W. Edwards Deming, also advocate participation by the workers in as much as possible of the decision making about workplace design and goals.

Management is as old as humankind, but has just become the subject of serious study during the last 100 years.

The 1970's brought an import of so-called Quality Circle concepts from Japan where they'd blossomed from American teachings after World War II. The Japanese, under the reconstruction "guidance" of American academics, were willing learners. Their culture was more tuned in to group decision making. The idea of quality control circles was to encourage discussion and suggestions from operational employees. Most American businesses in the 1970's were still operating in an authoritarian management style.

So, in the 1970's, it became necessary to teach workers, not just managers, the process by which problems are analyzed and decisions are made. Where workers were expected to provide and support suggestions to management on product design and production issues, they needed the skills that had formerly been restricted to management. The tools in this book are frequently taught to Quality Circle Teams, Continuous Improvement Teams, Total Quality Management or Participative Management operations by whatever name. But it was another decade or two before this participation moved from the technical areas into management areas.

The 1990's brought more business and organizational acceptance of the concept of self-managed work teams. These teams are the next step beyond classic Quality Circles, in that the decisions they're asked to make include not only the technical aspects of the product or service, but the managerial aspects as well. Self-managed work teams can take on such tasks as product or service design and problem solving, as did Quality Circles. But they also may take on managerial types of tasks including scheduling, employee evaluation, hiring, compensation, and many others which were formerly the sole responsibility of management. The effective use of teams is very briefly discussed in Chapter Six.

Other business changes in the 1990's included increased internationalization of businesses, increased rate and frequency of changes in nearly everything, more fragmentation of the workplace, shifting job patterns, and a greater emphasis on productivity through a variety of techniques from automation to offshoring to re-engineering. The effects of these changes are also discussed very briefly in Chapter Six.

Management Today

Today's employees and teams require many of the same skills as their managers, namely decision making and problem solving skills. The diagram below indicates that in today's organizations, even the lowest level employees spend some of their time doing things like planning, organizing, problem solving, decision making, and so on. Note that under the old style, the lowest level employees spent 100% of their time using their technical skills, but today they spend at least some time doing these things which had been previously thought of as "management" skills.

Old vs. New Management Skills

Type of Skills Needed

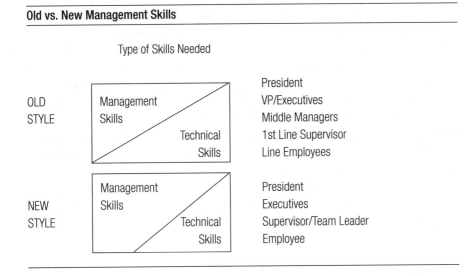

One of the most common structures used to teach and learn management processes is the one developed by Henri Fayol. His description of what managers do has been reworded in many current texts to include at least the four functions of ***Planning, Organizing, Directing, and Controlling***. Discussions of management may also include such other functions or activities as ***staffing, leading, communicating, motivating, delegating, etc.***, as separate and perhaps equal functions to the four listed above.

Nearly all of the functions in any description of management require decision making and problem solving in order to be done successfully. As explained earlier, this book deals mainly with the planning and control aspects of management.

The next chapter details the steps by which planning and control are accomplished by managers. This discussion prepares the way for the introduction of decision making and problem solving in Chapter Three.

Summary

Management often appears to be just common sense, yet it is really a very complex process. Perhaps the most important tasks in managing are problem solving and making decisions. These are the subject of this text, and they are the processes by which management happens.

Everyone makes decisions, but all kinds of decisions have a common structure. It is this structure or process which the text analyzes so that we can improve our skills in making decisions. This analysis begins with a look at the "big picture" -- a very brief history of management.

Management has been around since the earliest people, but has only been studied as a process during the last hundred years or so. Early efforts focused on structuring and quantitatively evaluating the tasks involved with management and production, but the Hawthorne Studies taught us that understanding people and groups may be even more important than a task orientation. Recent developments in participative management make it important for the processes of decision making and problem solving to be understood by all levels of employees of an organization, rather than just by the managers.

All of the functions of management are interrelated, and most require some amount of decision making and problem solving. Those specific skills are detailed in Chapter Three.

Study Questions

1. Which of the functions of management, as defined by Fayol, require problem solving and decision making skills?
2. How long has management existed, and when did we first start to study it seriously?
3. Identify several of the major contributors to management thought during the past century.

4. How are quality circles of the 1970's & 80's different from the newer self-managed work teams?

5. Why is the understanding of decision making and problem solving skills more important today than it was a hundred or even twenty years ago?

Exercise

List several decisions you've had to make and several problems you've had to solve at work or in your personal life. These will form the basis for the discussion of the steps in decision making and problem solving in the next chapter.

CHAPTER 2

Management Planning and Control

*"Cheshire Puss, would you tell me, please, which way I ought to walk
from here?"*
"That depends a good deal on where you want to get to," said the Cat.
"I don't much care where —" said Alice.
"Then it doesn't matter which way you walk," said the Cat.
"— so long as I get <u>somewhere</u>," Alice added as an explanation.
"Oh, you're sure to do that," said the Cat, "if only you walk long enough."
– Lewis Carroll

Chapter Objectives:

This chapter is designed to enable the reader to ....

- list and describe the steps in the planning process.
- list and describe the steps in the control process.
- understand the different classifications of plans.
- understand the different classifications of controls.
- explain three different classifications of management tools.
- understand how planning & controlling relate to the other management functions.

I n the last chapter, we learned that a way of describing management using Henri Fayol's concept is to envision it as composed of different functions or activities. These include planning, organizing, directing, controlling and — depending on the model to which you subscribe — maybe several other things as well.

The steps in Planning and Control are described in detail in this chapter, and we also look at how the other functions of management tie into the management process.

The Steps in the Planning Process

Everything in history which has been planned was done so in a highly predictable pattern. Whether you attempt to plan the introduction of a new product, a company picnic, your career, how to start up a business, how to win a baseball game, or any other definable event or activity, you will go through a six step process. These steps are:

Steps in the Planning Process

1. Establish goals or objectives	4. Evaluate options
2. Define limits	5. Choose the best option(s)
3. Develop options	6. Implement or Recycle to a more specific level

The next few pages will help you to understand each of these six steps.

Step 1: Establish Your Goals or Objectives

You must define what you want to have happen before you can build a plan to make it happen. The cliché for this warns you, "If you don't know where you're going, you'll never know if you've arrived." (There's also, of course, the implication of the chapter-opening quote.) Therefore, the first stage in planning is to establish your goals.

Goals are usually seen as more global ideas, while objectives are more precise, measurable and specific. They are means to the end; things you must do to achieve a goal. Frankly, the distinction may fade in practice. The theoretical differences between goals and objectives are discussed *ad nauseum* in a variety of management books. (Some are listed in the bibliography.) Regardless of the specifics, what we're dealing with here is a relatively simple idea: ***What do you want to happen?***

Effective goals — i.e., ones which can be used successfully for planning — need to be specific, measurable, and valid. **Specific** means that the goal details exactly what is to be accomplished. **Measurable** means that a manager can tell whether or not a goal has been achieved. **Valid** means that the goal is actually something that needs to happen in order for the larger plan or the organization as a whole to be successful.

Step 2: Define Your Limits

Limits, also called parameters or conditions, are usually stated in terms of what resources the decision maker or the management of the organization is willing and able to apply toward the achievement of the objectives. Therefore, when defining limits you need to ask such questions as:

- How much time before the goal should be reached?
- How much money can be put towards its achievement?
- What equipment or facilities are available?
- What technological capabilities can be tapped?
- What people can be used?
- What technical and managerial skills do they have?
- What other resources are necessary?
- What will affect progress toward the goal?

The purpose of thinking through the limits is to reduce the number of options to be considered in the next step. For example, if your objective was to travel from Cincinnati to Chicago, there are millions of ways this could be done. You could go by car, bicycle, plane, train, bus, or canoe. You could go through Indianapolis or Seattle or Paris.

By listing the limits before considering these alternatives, you reduce your pool of options to a practical number of ones which will ultimately be viable. You could list limits such as: (1) getting there within one day and (2) having your own car to drive upon arrival. This, then, makes you limit your choice of options to the various fairly direct highway routes.

Even when you know what you want to happen, many ingredients may be needed

An important word of caution goes with this step: **Don't overdo the limits!** Too many limits reduce the potential for some creative options. Also, the limits may begin to focus you too early toward some conscious or unconscious preconceived best way to accomplish your goal.

You need to set limits, but only essential and absolute ones. For example, if you say "*MY* car," rather than "*A* car," above, you've limited yourself much more. If you just need "A car" upon arrival, then going by plane, train, boat, or hitchhiking are still realistic options if you buy, rent or borrow a car in Chicago. They might also be better or cheaper options, even with the additional cost of getting a car in Chicago.

Step 3: Develop Your Options

Step three is the very important *inductive* or creative part of the planning process. It must be done effectively — i.e., you must come up with a good list of options from which to choose — in order to come up with a good plan.

A discussion of ways you can develop creative options is put off until Chapter Four. However, two important points need to be covered here:

(1) **Complete step three before you even think about step four,** and

(2) **It's very seldom practical to come up with *all possible* options, nor is it usually necessary.**

There are several important reasons to isolate step three from step four. For one thing, they use different sides of the brain. Creativity is generally associated with the right side of the brain, while analysis skills are resident in the left side of the brain. Further, many of the tools discussed later in this text are associated exclusively with one step or the other. Jumping back and forth between these steps adds unnecessary complications to the planning process particularly if you are working with a group. Finally, human nature isn't always as patient as it should be. Flip flopping between these steps will add time and probably increase pressures to cut the process short. The moral is: don't start to evaluate the options until you've come up with an adequate list of options.

What is an "adequate" list? It is one which (a) has been developed with enough thought that you've included several different kinds of options. This may mean different vendors or locations or styles, etc. And (b) the differences between options should be more than just cosmetic. For example, if your house looks dreary, your decision choices should not be only between brands of white paint. They should include various colors, stain, aluminum siding and bricks. Of course you might eliminate some of these in the next step, but at least consider them.

> *Planning must be done in two stages: Steps 1–3, then Steps 4–6. You can't jump back and forth between Steps 3 and 4.*

To illustrate the hazard of jumping to step four without first completing step three, consider the process of planning to buy a car: *Objective*: To buy a car by this Friday. *Limits*: $18,000; Need room for five passengers; 4-wheel drive; Etc. (add limits to meet your personal needs).

If you go to the first dealer's lot, see a car that fits the limits, and buy it without looking elsewhere, you may not have implemented the best plan. As you drive home in your new car, you may pass other dealerships and wonder if some of those cars might have been cheaper or better.

The other rule of thumb is not to go to step four until you have a minimum of four viable options. If they're coming fairly easily, go for a dozen. Continuing with the example of buying a car: Unless you live in a very small town a long way from anywhere else you might buy a car, you'll probably not consider every possible option before you make a choice. Somewhere between dozens and thousands of cars are for sale in most places. It's neither possible nor logical to check out each and every one before you buy.

> *Don't limit your options too much or too soon. Use limits which eliminate only extreme options.*

How many options are enough? It depends on the nature of the decision. This subject is treated in more detail in chapter three, but the range of four to twelve options is adequate for most planning. Chapter Five and the tools in Chapter Nine will introduce you to a variety of ways to create a broader and more effective list of options.

Step 4: Evaluate Your Options

This is the **deductive** or data gathering and analytical (i.e., the left brain) part of the planning process.

Probably no option is perfect. Each will have pros and cons. These pros and cons will be of different importance in the evaluation. You'll have to collect data on each option. How much information you need and where to get it depends, of course, on

The key ingredient in success is a well designed plan.

what sort of decision you're making. To continue with the example of buying an automobile, let's say that you've narrowed it down to six possible choices. All of these fit the price, size and four wheel drive limits you set in step three. Now you must gather and analyze further information on each of them. You'll probably have several sources for this information. One would be the cars themselves. You will probably test drive them, kick the tires and smell the upholstery. Another might be the salesperson. Still others would be publications such as *Consumer Reports* or similar ones which objectively evaluate automobiles. Also, your insurance agent, Uncle Harry, your spouse, and Joe (owner of Joe's Garage, who currently holds the mortgage to your house based on your previous repair bills) may also contribute to your evaluation.

For a different sort of an example, let's say you're trying to hire a new employee. *Goal*: Hire an electrical engineer. *Limits*: $42,000 maximum salary; able to start work first of the month; must know about the industrial controls business. *Options*: Through advertising and employment agency contacts, you have received applications from seven candidates.

Now you must evaluate these options (applicants). Undoubtedly, you'll find pros and cons to each prospective employee. You'll have to collect further data on each of the seven, probably from several sources, and evaluate this data before you can make your decision.

Later chapters will introduce a variety of tools and techniques to help you effectively review the list of options you've created and establish an objective, methodical means of evaluating each.

Step 5: Choose the Best Option(s)

The results of your evaluation in step four may lead you to an obvious choice. On the other hand, there may be no obvious choice. While some narrowing of the field of options and further data collection may help, the fact of the matter is that most decisions are based on calculated risks. The subject of risk is also covered in a later chapter.

At some point, you will probably decide. You may decide not to decide, which is still a decision. Or you may procrastinate until the decision is irrelevant or your options disappear or the Cleveland Indians win the World Series. The latter is probably not good management – fewer than 5% of the people alive today had been born when that happened (unless they get lucky this year). Even Moses made a decision after only forty years. So now that you've chosen the best way to achieve the objective or goal you started out with in step one, it's time to put this choice into effect.

Step 6: Implement (or) Recycle to a More Specific Level

This step is an "either/or," and depends on how broad the goal or objective was in step one.

If the decision requires no further thought of great consequence, you can implement it. For example, if you've decided which engineering candidate you want to hire, do it. If you've decided which route to take from Cincinnati to Chicago, go for it. These decisions may be low-level enough that almost no further planning is needed before you can put them into effect.

But perhaps your goal in step one was that you wanted to go into business for yourself. Maybe your limits in step two were the $50,000 you just inherited from Uncle Abner's will and your own job skills. Your step three options could have included opening up a shoe store, buying a pizza franchise, and starting a computer maintenance service. Your evaluation of these and others in step four included the potential profit for each, competition, legal issues, etc., and your step five choice was to open a shoe store.

Opening a shoe store is not a plan which can be implemented right away. It needs to be supplemented with a number of other, lower-level plans. This means you'll have to go back through the planning process several times. The decision of opening a shoe store has now become the new goal or objective for further planning. You need to plan where to open the store. You need to plan how to advertise. You need to plan how to organize and staff the operation of the store. You need to plan how to obtain inventory. You may need to plan how to obtain further financing, etc.

Results of Plans which are developed for broad objectives are new, lower level objectives, rather than things which can be immediately implemented.

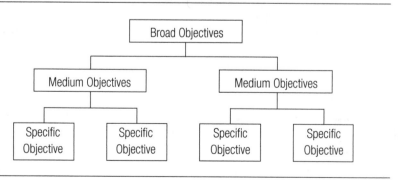

So, you recycle. A new, lower level, more specific goal is to find a location for your shoe store. Limits would include geographic distribution of customers, costs of various locations (and whether to purchase or rent), etc. To determine your options, you call a commercial Realtor or go through one or more of the processes in Chapter Five. Your evaluation of the options might be done using one or more of the tools described later in this book. Your choice of a location may be a low enough level decision that you can just sign a lease to implement it. But you still have other specific plans to make on personnel, inventory, additional financing, etc.

Different Kinds of Plans

While all plans go through the same steps, there are different categories of plans. Details of these are covered in principles of management texts, but common categorization systems for plans include:
- Strategic plans (broad) versus Operational or Tactical plans (specific)
- Long Range plans (probably at least a year) versus Short Range (ten seconds to one year)
- Standing plans (such as policies, rules, etc.) versus Single Purpose plans (one-time, unique)

It's not the purpose of this book to get into the finer points of these classifications. Refer to the bibliography or nearly any management textbook if you're interested in more details on this subject.

The next process to discuss is the management function of **control**.

Steps in the Control Process

The plans that you've created will provide the basis and a starting point for control processes. The purpose of the control process in management is to make certain that you (i.e., the person, organization or group which has made the plan) are actually achieving the objectives established in the plan.

Like planning, control also has specific, definable steps which will happen regardless of what type of control we're dealing with. It could be quality control, production control, inventory control, controlling your temper, or any other type of control you can imagine. The steps will always include: (1) *Establishing the standards*, (2) *Measuring performance*, (3) *Comparing the performance to the standards and evaluat-*

ing whether or not they're being met, and finally, (4) if they're not being met, *Analyze the cause of and correct the deviation from standards.*

Steps in the Control Process

---

1. Establish standards
2. Measure performance
3. Compare performance to standards; evaluate
4. Analyze cause of and correct deviations

Each of these steps will be discussed in turn.

Step 1: Establish standards

The standards in a control process normally flow out of the planning and decision making done earlier. Good standards, like good goals & objectives, are measurable, specific, and serve a purpose in the control process.

To help understand the variety of standards which might apply to various control processes, we will use three examples. The first is a quality control, the second is a production control, and the third is what most people would call rules.

Type of Standard	Example	Specifications	Measurement Tool
Quality Control	Size of Ball Bearings	1.000" plus or minus 0.003"	Micrometer or other physical tool
Production Control	Sales Quotas	25 units per week	Sales Reports
Policies & Rules	Waiter's Appearance	Wear tuxedo Wash hands	Manager's Observation

A standard needed to control the quality of ball bearings could specify that each unit must be 1.000" ± .003". This comes out of the plan, which was probably to provide a product which the customer will buy or which will be usable in a machine being built. If the ball bearings are larger than 1.003" or smaller than 0.997", they won't be acceptable.

If a company plans to sell a certain number of iPods or washing machines, the standard might be in the form of a quota for the sales staff. Perhaps, for our plan to succeed it was computed that each sales person must sell 25 units per week.

*All sorts
of events
require
control.*

In the operation of an exclusive restaurant, one of the standards which might come out of the plan is to have the waiters wearing tuxedos. The health department, in order for the restaurant to stay open, might require the cooks to wash their hands upon arrival for work. Rules, you say? Yes, but standards, too.

Step 2: Measure performance

Measurement requires tools of some kind. You can measure the approximate size of your driveway using the length of your foot as the measuring tool. On the other hand, if you need to find out what size belt to buy for your cousin Larry's birthday gift, a measurement more precise than your foot would be appropriate (unless you have a strange relationship with Larry).

So the tool has to fit the nature of the standard you've set. To measure the ball bearings, a micrometer or a laser measuring device might be the tool of choice. (A micrometer is a precise, physical kind of measuring tool.) Tighten it on a sample ball bearing, then read the scale.

But a physical tool does nothing for measuring the second example standard, the sales quota. To find out whether or not 25 units were sold last week, a report of some kind is needed. It could be from the salesperson, or it could be from some objective source such as the order entry department or the accounting department.

And a report seems useless to measure performance in the third example. It's illogical to have the waiters fill out weekly reports stating whether or not they wore a tuxedo, nor will the cooks report they forgot to wash their hands twice this month. The only way to effectively measure performance on these standards is through a manager's observation. The manager must look around to see that either the waiters have on tuxedos or they don't; that cooks, upon arrival or return from break, either head for the sink or they don't.

So the measurement tools can take many forms, including simple observation, reports, complex analyses, and physical measurements. The only constant is that the tool must be able to tell the manager whether or not the standard has been met.

Step 3: Compare Performance to Standards and Evaluate

Now that we know what our results **should be** and what they **are**, we need to compare these two levels. The results will typically be reported in the form of "Yes," it is in control, or "No," it's not in control, or some percentage of variation from the established standard.

Sometimes immediate action is needed to put out "brushfires"!

If the answer is "Yes," or the variation is minor and within the limits we set, the process is performing as planned. It is *in control*. When this happens, we can be happy and reward the workers, put yellow smile stickers all around, or at least go do something else until we need to check it again.

If measurement and comparison tell us the process is *not in control*, we must go further and evaluate WHY the process is not operating as planned. This requires problem solving (deductive) skills.

Ways of finding out why performance is not meeting standards vary according to the process being controlled. In some cases the answers may be very obvious, but others may take a great deal of detective work. Some specific suggestions on ways to evaluate why standards aren't being met are covered in later chapters.

Returning to the example standards from step one, assume they've turned up *out of control*. First, what if the ball bearings are coming out with an average size of 1.009"? It's not enough to just know that they're out of control, because several things might be causing that, and correcting the problem depends on the cause. Perhaps they are too large because they're supposed to be tumbled in a polishing barrel which would take off the mold seams and whittle them down to size. Maybe they are being taken out of that too soon, or the abrasive in the barrel needs to be replaced. On the other hand, it could be because the alloy steel used to make them is the wrong chemical composition. It may not respond as expected to the heating or abrasion. Or, the problem may be due to several causes all at once!

The sales person might have sold only 19 washing machines this week because a competitor had a special sale going on. It could also be that she or he only was at work four days due to illness. It could be that the machines were on backorder, and customers wouldn't wait.

Waiters might have shown up without their tuxedos because they forgot to have them cleaned or because none was issued to them. The cooks may have forgotten the rule or don't believe the rule is important, or the water may have been shut off by the city due to a billing problem.

So it's not just knowing the standard wasn't met. Managers also have to determine WHY it wasn't met so that the last step can be accomplished. *Without the last step, it's not*

Part of the final step in control is to attempt to prevent the problem from recurring.

a control process; it's just a measurement. In order to truly be a management control process, it must correct the deviation and reduce its chance of happening again.

Step 4: Analyze Causes of and Correct Any Deviations from Standards

This step is only necessary when the comparison in step three shows the process to be out of control. What it takes to accomplish this step totally depends on the results of the evaluation in step three. Step four amounts to implementing the decision which came out of the problem solving process just completed. Here are some possible correction steps for the three examples which have been used.

If the ball bearings are too large because they were not tumbled long enough, change the timing. If it's lack of abrasive, fix that. If it's the wrong steel, contact the supplier for an adjustment.

If the sales were off due to competition, rethink the market strategy. If it was illness, consider alternative ways to get the sales made. If it was inventory shortages, find a way to keep the problem from recurring.

If the waiter and cooks could have prevented the problem, appropriate discipline should be applied (warning, then suspension, then termination for successive violations). If it was beyond their control, determine why and what must be done to keep it from happening again.

Different Kinds of Controls

All controls follow the same steps, but there are various ways of categorizing controls, just as there were with plans.

More sophisticated control systems are self-correcting, or **closed-loop**. One of the simplest examples of a closed loop control is your furnace or air conditioning system using a thermostat. If it gets too cold, the furnace is turned on or the air conditioning turned off. When the temperature reaches the appropriate level, the system again adjusts automatically. Control systems which don't have this automatic correction require the intervention of a person. They are called **open loop** systems.

Control systems can also be classified according to how quickly the comparison to standards happens. The feedback on standard versus actual can be somewhat delayed, concurrent, or even anticipatory. A manager who gets only monthly reports on the budget is receiving **delayed feedback**. He or she may not know whether the allocation in the budget has been exceeded until the report has come out. Corrective action then can only deal with the subsequent month's budget. While this is better than not knowing, it is the least useful form of information.

If the manager has a computer and access to the budget data each time an expenditure is authorized, then **concurrent (or "real time") feedback** is possible. There is an immediate knowledge on whether or not the allocations have been exceeded. This is more expensive than delayed feedback.

A budget package which shows information on both the percentage of allocation spent and the percentage of the month spent is a very simple type of **forward-looking** control. If the budget for the month is 70% spent and we're only 40% of the way through the month, that indicates to the manager that things will be out of control unless some corrective action is taken now to

Working without tools makes it difficult to achieve the desired objective.

reduce expenditures for the rest of the month. Other controls can be established which predict that the process will go out of control if present trends continue. Forward-looking controls are usually more expensive to establish than other types. They may still be cost effective, however. More can be learned about these in books on management.

One final concept related to control is **Management by Exception**, often called **MBE**. In simplified terms, this means that a manager should not over control the work place. Once controls are set up, let the processes run with only minimal checking. Colloquially speaking, "If it ain't broke, don't fix it." Only when exceptions arise — i.e., the standards are not being met — should management intervene.

Forward looking controls are more expensive to set up, but may cost less in the long run because they reduce the number of times a process gets out of control.

Planning & Control Related to Other Management Functions

Planning and control are only two of the functions of management. Planning requires anticipating problems and making decisions for the future. Control requires solving problems when performance doesn't meet standards.

This book, as promised, won't deal with the details of organizing, staffing, directing, and other management functions. Briefly, though, here are some other examples to indicate how decision making and problem solving are also related to those activities.

As we accomplish any of the management functions, we're really making decisions — implementing plans — to meet objectives we've established in each of those areas. The earlier example in step four of planning (page 16) showed how we might go about staffing a position.

Consider how we decide on the design of an organization structure:

- **Set objective:** To organize our business in the most effective manner.
- **Define limits:** The employees, their skills and resources we have available.
- **Develop options:** Possible organization structures include traditional, matrix, centralized, divided by function, tall or flat, etc.
- **Evaluate options:** Consider the pros and cons of each option.
- **Choose best:** The traditional, flat, centralized might be the best, given the conditions in a particular company. Or it might be matrix, or whatever.
- **Implement:** Post it on the wall and tell people that's how it works in this organization.

Just as all other management functions require planning & decision making, they also require control. Control can be applied to staffing, for example. If the organization has hired too many people who quit or are let go after only a few months, the staffing process may be out of control. It can be evaluated by asking, "What were the standards expected from the staffing process? What was the performance? Did it meet the standard? If people are leaving at too high a rate, why? How do we correct it?"

Completing the Management Cycle

Sometimes we find, as a result of our efforts at control, that our planning was flawed in some way. The "output" of the control process then becomes "input" for the next round of planning by the manager or team.

Planning and control have a lot in common. They each have predictable steps which occur no matter what process is being planned and controlled. The output of the planning process dictates the standards in control of that process. The output or results of the control may influence future plans about the process.

Certain aspects of management may be circular: The output of one is the input to the next. Also, certain tools may be useful for more than one aspect of management.

In fact, many of the tools used in planning are exactly the same ones used in control. (Several of these are discussed in Chapter Eight.) **Budgets**, for example, are tools which are used for both planning and control.

As it's being constructed, a budget is a plan. How much money will come in for the month? How will it be spent? As a budget is prepared, a manager goes through the six steps discussed under planning. Once the budget is completed and approved, it becomes a control tool. Each of the four steps listed under control happens. The standard comes from the approved budget, performance is checked against the standard, an evaluation is made, and deviations are corrected as necessary. If you overspent your personal budget on groceries, you may have to give up going to the show. If an organization overspent its budget on payroll, it may have to delay equipment purchases.

Many other tools are like that. Gantt charts and PERT Charts, also described in Chapter Eight of this book, are planning tools which help managers or teams to think through each of the steps necessary in a major project. Once completed, they're excellent control tools which help manage the project much more efficiently.

Different Types of Management Tools

We've referred to "tools" quite a few times in the first part of this book. It might be good to define what is meant by the word *tool.*

A tool is an aid to accomplishing a task. Most of us are accustomed to thinking of tools in a physical sense, such as a hammer or saw. Management tools are a bit different, but the definition still fits. Some management tools are con-

Tools which are not properly designed will not be helpful.

cepts, some are **models**, and a few are **physical**. Still, their purpose is to aid managers in accomplishing tasks.

Concepts are ways of looking at things that provide a structure for analysis. You have probably used a template or a stencil to help you draw circles or squares or consistently sized letters. A concept does the same thing for your thinking. An example of a conceptual management tool with which you may be familiar is Brainstorming (described in Chapter Nine). The brainstorming process provides a template for thinking — a way of doing it that helps achieve consistent results. Accounting is another conceptual tool.

> *If your only tool is a hammer, you tend to see all problems as nails. Having a versatile, well stocked toolbox is essential for a good manager.*

Models are simplifications of reality in order to help us better understand reality. For example, if you were trying to explain an airplane to someone who didn't know what one looked like or how it worked, a model might be helpful. You can get 25 cent models of a plane out of the gumball machines in the Wal-Mart lobby, or you can get ones that cost hundreds of dollars, actually fly, and are scaled quite accurately. They both may help explain an airplane, but the more sophisticated your explanation, the more precise your model needs to be and the closer it will approach reality. That's an example of a physical model. Managers often need conceptual models. Examples of conceptual models for decision making and problem soving include queuing theory (explained in Chapter Ten) and EOQ (also Chapter Ten) and many other tools covered later in this book.

Physical management tools are such things as computers. They are also extremely useful and knowing how to use them could make applying the concepts and models easier and quicker. However, they are not the subject of this book.

There are lots of more sophisticated tools (check your local MBA provider), and many that are less sophisticated than the ones included here. The tools chosen for this book range from very simple to modestly complex.

Like any good toolbox, there is a variety of choices. If your only tool is a hammer, then you treat all problems like nails. Unless you match the tool you use with the problem you're solving, you may wind up doing more harm than good. The mix of tools in the book will give you something that might work on nearly any kind of problem or decision you face.

Management tools can be further categorized into: **Inductive** and **Deductive.**

Inductive tools are useful in certain steps of the planning and controlling processes. They help us move from the specific to the general. When faced with decisions and problems, we want to create a variety of options to be considered before we begin to choose from among them. Inductive tools, then, are creative aids. Brainstorming is an inductive tool.

Deductive tools are useful in other steps of the planning and controlling processes. They are more objective and analytical, moving us from the general to the specific. The deductive tools help to objectively analyze possible causes or options to choose the best option or determine the most likely cause. Queuing theory is a deductive tool.

But even a properly designed tool will not guarantee you success!

Chapter Eight introduces four tools related to Planning and Control. You may wish to skip to that chapter now, or just continue with the next chapter in this theory portion of the book.

Summary

The planning process has six steps. They are: (1) Establish Goals; (2) Define Limits; (3) Determine Options; (4) Evaluate Options; (5) Choose; and (6) Implement or Recycle. These steps may take only a second or two for a simple decision such as which pair of socks to wear today, or many months for complex decisions such as how to enter a new product market. Brief or extended, the same six steps will always be followed. A key point in this process is to clearly separate steps three and four, since they require different types of thinking and different tools.

The control process has four steps. They are: (1) Establish Standards; (2) Measure Performance; (3) Compare to Standards and Evaluate; and (4) Analyze Cause of and Correct Deviations from Standard. Again, the complexity of control processes will vary, but the steps will be constant. Step four must happen in order to have a true control process. The most difficult step is step three, since it requires problem solving to determine the causes of variation from standard, and therefore, what corrective action to take. Control techniques can be classified according to their timeliness, that is whether they provide comparison to standards after, during or before occurrence of the variation from standard.

Other traditional functions of management require planning and control, as well as decision making and problem solving. More will be explained regarding the specific decision making and problem solving processes in Chapter Three.

Human beings have developed a number of tools to help them with their complex jobs, and management is no exception. These tools are aids to accomplishing a task. The ones in this text can be categorized as concepts or models, and as inductive or deductive.

Study Questions

1. What are the characteristics of an effective goal or objective?
2. Name some examples of limits as the term applies to the planning process.
3. Why is it important to separate the third and fourth steps in the planning process?
4. What is meant by "Recycle" as one of the possible options in the sixth step of planning?
5. Explain where control standards come from.
6. List some different types of measurement tools.
7. Explain how planning and control are integral parts of the other functions of management.
8. Distinguish between concepts and models.
9. Distinguish between deductive tools and inductive tools.

Exercises

- Describe what would be included in each of the planning steps if you are planning a birthday party.
- What sort of standards might be set if you were trying to control the planting and growth of a garden?

3

Decision Making and Problem Solving

"More than any time in history, mankind faces a crossroads. One path leads to despair and utter hopelessness, the other to total extinction. Let us pray that we have the wisdom to choose correctly."

– Woody Allen

Chapter Objectives:

This chapter is designed to enable the reader to ....
- Understand why a structure for decision making is important.
- List and explain the steps in decision making.
- Describe when decision making is required.
- Explain how to determine a decision's importance.
- List and explain the steps in problem solving.
- Describe when problem solving is required.

D ecision making is the skill that makes management "happen." Without decision making, no management has occurred. Problem solving can be done by non-managers, but it, too, is an excellent skill for managers to have. This chapter presents an underlying framework and process by which we can analyze all decision making and problem solving events. In dealing with anything which is complex, an understanding of the basic structure can be enormously beneficial.

First, it can give us confidence that we can handle the situation.

Second, it can provide a discipline to follow, preventing false starts and the need for retracing our steps. We know what should be done first, then next, and so on. If we run into trouble, we know what tools or techniques might help us get back on track.

Finally, it can allow us to concurrently develop the information and support necessary to get management, peers or others buy into an idea – something further covered in Chapter Seven.

While nearly all problems and decisions will contain the steps explained in this chapter, there's no promise that they'll be as neat and clean (and obvious) as this structure suggests. In fact, these steps may be convoluted and obscure!

Nevertheless, the structure is important because it provides a basis to begin from or to return to as you go about the decision making and problem solving processes.

Decision Making as a Process

All of us make many decisions each day, ranging from what to have for breakfast and what clothes to wear, down to whether to watch the late night news and what time to set the alarm clock to wake us tomorrow. Barry Schwartz, in his engaging book *The Paradox of Choice – Why More is Less* discusses the challenges we face as we attempt to live our day to day lives in a society rife with choice. Very few people would agree with the premise of the famous quote attributed to Henry Ford regarding consumer choice: "They can have any color they want, as long as they want black." Most of us want more choice; but when is more too much? Mr. Schwartz mentions that in his modest-sized neighborhood grocery store, he found 285 varieties of cookies. Is that too many?

Most decisions that we make on a daily basis are relatively simple and automatic. How significant are the consequences for choosing the wrong cookie from among the 285? (Admittedly, they may be more serious if you have a two-year old.) Therefore, we usually don't consciously go through as extensive a process for what to have for breakfast as we do for buying a new car or opening a new business. That's because simple decisions don't require an analysis of the process.

However, bringing the steps of the process into conscious thought allows us to do as Frederick Taylor did with the coal shoveling study described in Chapter One. Studying the "common sense process" step by step can improve success.

Theorists speak of *Programmed* and *Non-Programmed* decisions. Programmed decisions are ones which are expected and for which there are precedents. Non-programmed decisions arise unexpectedly and require new processing of information.

Making decisions is a subordinate part of planning, problem solving and control. You must decide on goals and objectives. You must decide on allocation of resources. You must decide which is the best from among the options you've identified. You must decide what standards are necessary and what methods of correcting variation from standards are most appropriate.

The Steps in Decision Making

All decision making follows the same basic steps. They are:

Steps in Decision Making

1. Determine that a decision is needed.
2. Determine that decision's importance.
3. Assess what limits apply to the decision.
4. Determine possible choices.
5. Gather information about these possible choices.
6. Evaluate or test the possible choices.
7. Decide and Implement the decision.

Planning can be viewed as simply making decisions for the future.

Looking back to Chapter Two, the "steps in planning" include some similar-sounding phrases.

Why? Planning could be viewed as simply "making decisions for the future". Therefore, the steps are nearly the same. Sometimes we're deciding for right now, and sometimes we're planning — deciding for the future. The only difference is that we've divided the first step from Chapter Two into two parts.

Later in this chapter, another list of steps, this time for the problem solving process, again will include some similar items. Actually, the process of problem solving requires two decision making efforts: the first to determine the cause of the problem; the second to determine what should be done about it.

Some of the steps in decision making are better covered elsewhere, but a few require understanding before we get into the other subjects.

Step 1: Determine That a Decision Is Needed

Decisions are needed in order for things to happen in an orderly way. If you are responsible for making something happen, you must make decisions. A few questions you might want to ask yourself in this stage are:

- *Does it have to be decided?* What will happen if no decision is made? Often the answer is nothing. What pros and cons are there for inaction? Sometimes minor issues die a natural death if ignored, and no one cares. If that's the case, you can save yourself time and energy by not deciding.
- *Do I have the authority and/or power to make and implement the decision?* If not, why are you involved? Perhaps your reason for being involved is to recommend a course of action to someone else. Many staff people find themselves in this situation.
- *Do I have or can I get the necessary information to make the decision?* If not, you may as well throw a dart at a board with all the choices listed. No use agonizing over it if there's really no way to get the information on which of your options is better.
- *Who else could make it better?* Why don't they, then?

Step 2: Determine the Decision's Importance

Competent people intuitively know most of the time when decisions are important, and therefore merit more detailed processing of each of the steps. Dressing for a major job interview or social affair probably takes more thought than dressing to wash the car or the dog. Buying a house is a more important decision than buying socks.

Most of us, however, know some people who seem to have difficulty making these differentiations; persons who make all decisions seem nearly equally important. These people usually frustrate themselves and others. We'll leave the analysis of why some people have this problem to the specialists in human behavior. (Barry Schwartz does a good job of that in his book which was mentioned on page 30.) For now, we will consider some of the typical criteria most people use subconsciously to determine a decision's importance to them:

- *How much does it cost?* Importance usually increases with cost, but not always.
- *How long is the commitment?* Importance usually increases with the length of time with which one will have to endure the consequences.
- *Who is involved?* Importance usually increases directly with their numbers and significance to the decision maker.
- *Can it be changed later?* Importance usually increases with a "no."
- *How soon does it have to be made?* Urgency and accompanying stress usually increase as the deadline nears. In one sense, then, importance may also. However, a decision may be urgent but still not very important.
- *How much information is available to make the decision?* While this factor also may not directly influence importance of the decision, it is a consideration regarding the effort necessary to make the decision. Either extreme, too much or not enough information, may be stressful.

Occasionally, however, we all goof in our estimation of a decision's importance. We may think a decision unimportant that really is, or vice-versa. This usually happens because we weren't aware of or paying attention to all the data. And, of course, sometimes things change after we've begun the decision making process.

Step 3: Assess What Limits Apply to the Decision

The subject of Limits was treated in more detail in Chapter Two. As a reminder, limits are usually defined in terms of resources available: time, money, people, and so on. It's important to know at the start what these limits are so that the final decision will work. Also, recall that limits should be set sparingly.

Step 4: Determine Possible Choices

Both creativity and research skills may be necessary to do this effectively. This step and a variety of tools which may help you do it are included in later chapters. The "Develop Options" discussion in Chapter Two is relevant here, especially the rule of completing this step before going on to the next.

Step 5: Gather Information about the Choices

This step is covered in detail in Chapter Five. There, you'll learn how to determine such things as where to get information, how much information you need, and other important considerations.

Step 6: Evaluate or Test the Possible Choices

Once you've developed your list of possible actions and collected information about them, you need to assess which is best and/or whether any or all of them will work. Ideas on doing this are also covered in Chapter Five, and tools to help are included in Chapters Ten and Eleven.

Step 7: Decide and Implement the Decision

Making the decision may become easy if a clear best choice emerges. If not, you'll have to take some risk as you make the decision. Dealing with this and minimizing it are also covered in Chapter Five.

Now that the decision making process has been described, the next issue to be presented is problem solving.

Problem Solving as a Process

Nearly all human beings and many lower species solve problems every day. Just as was said about decision making, problem solving for any purpose will follow a predictable pattern. Even though we may not consciously be aware of it, certain steps will occur. For a simple problem, the time span will be almost instantaneous; for a complex one, it may take months or years - as medical research often does.

In this book, we want to focus on problem solving in businesses and organizations, but the process applies to any problem you may face in life. The process actually includes two rounds of decision making, which is why that topic was covered first.

Management requires problem solving in several different circumstances:

First, if an adequate number of options are not developed during the planning process. On these occasions, a goal has been identified, but how to achieve it — or a sufficient number of possible solutions — has not emerged. The problem solving here must address how to remove the creativity barrier.

Second, when standards are not being met in the control process. Several examples of this situation were given in Chapter Two when we discussed how to "compare to standards and evaluate." This is probably the more traditional point at which managers move into a problem solving mode.

Finally, when problems or opportunities arise independent of planning and control. Our planning can not be perfect. Conditions change and unexpected things happen. Sometimes these will also occasion the need for problem solving.

The Steps in the Problem Solving Process

Problem solving, like planning, control and decision making, involves consistent, specific and predictable steps. Many models of problem solving exist. Some have more or fewer steps or approach it from a different perspective. For purposes of discussion in this book, ten steps are used.

Steps in Problem Solving

1. State the facts	6. List possible solutions.
2. Determine the real problem	7. Evaluate possible solutions.
3. List possible causes.	8. Decide on the best solutions.
4. Evaluate possible causes.	9. Test that solution.
5. Determine most likely cause.	10. Implement the solution.

Again, there exists a significant similarity between parts of this process and both the planning process developed in Chapter One and the decision making process developed earlier in this chapter. For this reason, problem solving can use many of the same tools we've already mentioned. Later chapters will describe them in more detail.

The most obvious solutions aren't always the best.

Problem solving begins with cause-effect analysis, then goes through the decision making process twice. First, you must decide on the most likely cause of the problem, then on the best solution. Therefore, you have *two "creative" stages* (steps 3 and 6) a*nd two "analytical" stages* (steps 4 and 7). You must be capable of switching back and forth in both the side of your brain and the tools you use.

Once again, it is appropriate to go through each of the steps. Where the process has been significantly covered already, we'll not belabor it. However, a couple of the steps do deserve extended explanations at this point.

Step #1: State the Facts

We usually know that a problem exists since we see its *effect*. The effect may be that control standards are not being met or that no clear plan is emerging to meet our planning objectives.

Step one requires the problem solver to put down *in writing* what is known as "fact." This helps to clarify understanding of the situation. The facts need to be in writing to keep them clear and specific in the problem solvers' minds. Otherwise, the problem may become something of an "amorphous blob," as McCall and Kaplan describe it in their book *Realities of Managerial Decision Making.*

Always look for the second right answer — or maybe the third.

Frequently, managers find that the so-called "facts" change as they get more information on the problem. Yes, that does mean they were probably wrong in the original assessment. Gasp! Well, don't waste time justifying it ... just restate the "facts" to reflect the new information. After all, if all the information had been available in the first place, most likely there would not have been a problem to solve. So it's really ok. If it makes you feel better, you can head the list "Facts?"

A good way of handling this step of the problem solving process is to make some short lists. Two of these should be "facts" about:

- **What IS true regarding the problem at this point?** and
- **What IS NOT true regarding the problem at this point?**

If the problem is that standards are not being met, another list should specify:

- **If standards were being met before, what changed?**

Listing facts is important because managers often mistake one problem for another or believe that symptoms are really causes. Listing facts is an essential prelude to step two. Managers must make sure they work on the correct problem; otherwise, they may come up with answers that don't provide solutions. In other words, they may solve the wrong problem, or find a "solution" to a problem that doesn't really exist.

How can a manager not understand the problem? Let's say a manager is quite concerned about the work in her area not being accomplished. She may know for a fact that there is high absenteeism among her employees, so she has decided that high absenteeism is the cause of the work not getting done. However, this may only be a symptom of other, deeper problems.

People may really be absent because they know there aren't enough parts to do the job, and they'll just sit around or be sent home. Or they may be absent because the area is so dusty they're getting sick. In either case, the absenteeism isn't a cause. It may or may not be a contributing factor, but correcting it won't solve the real problem of substandard production.

If the manager starts out with the wrong assumption, she'll have to backtrack. She should list "high absenteeism" as a fact, nothing more. When she gets to step two, it will be important to know about the absenteeism. But some other facts will be needed also.

Step #2: Determine the Real Problem

It's important to begin by identifying the real problem. Since it isn't always obvious, the manager may have to make several tries before hitting on a path to pursue. Using cause - effect logic will help here (see Chapter Nine). We usually start with the effect, *i.e.*, what's not happening that should (or vice versa). The <u>effect</u> (the deviation from what we want) IS the <u>problem</u> which we must solve.

So, after listing the facts in step one, we test reality: If any of the facts or answers to questions in step #1 is inconsistent with the undesirable effect (the deviation or problem at hand), then either we don't have the REAL problem defined yet or the "fact" is wrong. We then have to backtrack to a cause of this effect and see if <u>it</u> is the problem. Keep looking for prior, more basic problems which, if solved, will eliminate the current undesirable effect.

Once the apparent basic problem is determined, move on to step three.

Step #3: List Possible Causes

This is the start of the first decision making cycle. The problem solver must creatively come up with a list of possible causes of the problem. Remember the advice on coming up with options from Chapter Two: Get a reasonable number of options before you begin step #4. Stopping too soon will inhibit your success. Always look for the second right answer, or maybe the third. Tools and processes described in subsequent chapters may be helpful.

Step #4: Evaluate Possible Causes

The problem solver must now move to the analytical mode. Information must be gathered and comparisons must be made. Some of the tools described in the tools chapters (Eight through Eleven) may be useful.

Step #5: Determine the Most Likely Cause

Now that the problem solver has information on various things which might be the cause, he or she must determine which is most likely.

It's possible, of course, that there may be more than one cause which will need to be addressed. If so, which real cause has the highest priority? Which needs to be solved the most? It probably is the one that needs to be worked on first.

Recall from page 33 the list of questions to determine the importance of the decision: How much money is involved?; How many people?; etc. Your priority setting of which probable cause to deal with first should include similar questions. You may also need to consider other things such as safety, ability to remedy the problem, and so on.

Sometimes group input can be helpful in improving decisions.

Step #6: List Possible Solutions

This is the creativity stage of the second decision making cycle. (See step three above, but substitute "solutions" for "causes".) Again, remember the advice from chapter one: work on getting a good list of options BEFORE you begin to evaluate them. Otherwise, you may spend resources trying to implement the wrong solution. Separate step six from step seven, and don't go on until you have a good list.

Step #7: Evaluate Possible Solutions

Here's the second analytical stage. Which of the possible solutions seems likely to work best? Again you need to gather data about each and determine whether it will work. If it will, set it aside and go on to the next one. If not, discard it and go on to the next. You should not stop evaluating your possibilities just because you found one which works. There may be others which would work even better.

Your first check on whether you have a true possible solution is whether or not it is in conflict with any of the facts from step one. Then, if you apply the possible solution, will it actually alter the effect (the variation from standard you were trying to fix or remove the barrier to planning you encountered)? If the solution fits with the facts and would possibly solve or reduce the problem, then list it as a good one, and go on to repeat the process with the next possible solution.

Step #8: Decide on the Best Solution

Out of all the options which survived your evaluation in step seven, which will work best? "Best," of course, might be in terms of fastest, cheapest, most acceptable to employees, or some other criterion. The terms *optimize* or *satisfice* are often used in cases where the true "best" solution can't be implemented for some reason.

Step #9: Test the Solution

If it solves the problem, great. You're done. If not, try a different option out of the list from step six. If none of them work, you need to back up in the process (redo step five, then four, then three, then two, then one) until you have some success. The more effectively you accomplish each of these steps, the less backtracking you're likely to have to do. It's a challenge. Kaplan and McCall refer to the process as iterative and convoluted. In a complex problem solving situation, it's rare to get things completely right the first time through, so you can anticipate multiple iterations of this process.

Step #10: Implement the Solution

The description of the last step reinforces that problem solving is not an exact science. Some of it will be by trial and error. Nevertheless, the importance of the structure presented here should not be underestimated. Even when decisions and problems are ill defined and changing, they are best approached by a consistent process. To do otherwise invites confusion and frustration.

Are decision making and problem solving really this difficult? Sometimes they are. Remember, we opened the chapter saying that all decision making and problem solving do follow similar patterns, but because their importance and complexity vary, you may be able to make decisions and solve problems in just a few seconds. That's a good thing; otherwise waiters would hand you a menu and not come back for ages. (That happens anyhow, so never mind.) Seriously, the steps above are followed nearly every time you make decisions or solve problems. Just like Frederic W. Taylor took the process of shoveling coal into a blast furnace and divided it into many steps so that they could be effectively analyzed, that's what we have done here.

Summary

Decision making and problem solving are important parts of nearly all aspects of management. This chapter presented theoretical frameworks which can be used to break down each of those processes into discrete steps. This structure allows a manager

But how do we put this into effect?

— or anyone making a decision or solving a problem — to approach it in a systematic way.

Everyone makes decisions, and the same basic thought process is used for each. Most of the decisions we make are of only minor consequence, so we make them without much conscious thought. For the important ones, though, an analysis of how to do it should be helpful. We can usually determine how important a decision is to us intuitively, but some specific questions may help clarify the issue. We also need to ask ourselves if the decision is really one we should make.

The seven steps in the decision making process were explored, though detailed explanations of several were put off until later chapters. The steps are: (1) Determine that a decision is needed, (2) Determine that decision's importance, (3) Assess what limits apply to the decision, (4) Determine the possible choices, (5) Gather information about these possible choices, (6) Evaluate or test the possible choices, and (7) Decide.

This chapter also described the process of problem solving. It consists of ten steps and begins with an emphasis on identifying the problem through stating facts and testing reality. Then two decision making processes are used, first to establish the most probable cause, and second to determine the best solution to resolve the cause. Finally, the chosen solution is tested and implemented.

Study Questions

1. Name three reasons why it's important to understand the structure of the decision making process.
2. List the steps in decision making.
3. List the steps in problem solving.
4. How do you determine the importance of a decision or problem?
5. Name three situations in which problem solving is required.
6. Why is writing down "facts" an important first step in problem solving?

Exercise

Think of a problem which you've recently solved. Can you recreate the process you used to solve it? Does it follow the steps listed in this chapter? Or did you skip over some or have to backtrack? ***See the worksheets available on the CD which is sold with this book.***

CHAPTER 4

Creating
Possibilities

"Trust yourself. You know more than you think you do."

– Benjamin Spock, M.D.

Chapter Objectives:

This chapter is designed to enable the reader to ....

- Understand the barriers to creativity.
- Explain how decision making and problem solving can be enhanced by creativity.
- List and explain several specific activities which can help persons and groups overcome the barriers to creativity.

"Creating." The very word implies some higher power. It is the process by which new or different things and ideas develop. It is something that most of us feel inadequately prepared to do. We don't have that higher power, that extra skill, that unique insight which allows us to exclaim "aha!" as a light bulb magically appears above our heads.

Or do we? Look around at the people society considers to be creative: Artists, advertising writers, inventors, journalists, or others. Thomas Edison was much admired for his dogged determination in the face of thousands of failures to reach his few, albeit important successes. He even claimed that, "Success is 1% inspiration and 99% perspiration."

What makes "creative" people that way? Can you and I learn to be creative? A variety of books and articles on the subject are listed in the bibliography of this text, but a short answer to the question, "Can I learn to be creative?" is "Yes".

People are creative either because they learned to be or because they somehow avoided developing (or being hampered by) the blocks to creativity which our society lays for us.

Barriers to Creativity

Perhaps it was in kindergarten, or certainly by first grade, that you learned that society doesn't always appreciate creativity. We must — to a point — limit our natural childlike tendencies to do things our own way. While this can be taught in ways that don't unnecessarily inhibit creativity, the usual pattern is simply to encourage conformity.

"Color within the lines, Johnny."
"No, Sally, frogs are not red and blue; they're green."
"If any of you have to go to the bathroom, raise your hand."
*(*I always wondered how that would help. –RV*)*

As we get older, we face more and more rules:

"Drive on the right side of the road."
"Work starts at 8:00 a.m."

Some rules (such as the one about driving) are obviously necessary for safety or for the functioning of society in an orderly way. Others, however, are not.

The most insidious barriers to creativity are those unnecessary blocks we place on ourselves for a variety of reasons.

J.L. Adams, in his classic book ***Conceptual Blockbusting***, lists six types of conceptual blocks which interfere with our ability to explore and manipulate ideas, *i.e.*, to be creative. They are:

Conceptual Blocks to Creativity According to J.L. Adams

Emotional	Perceptual	Cultural
Environmental	Intellectual	Expressive

Adams, of course, describes each of these in more detail, but here's a brief synopsis of each:

Emotional Blocks. Examples of emotional blocks include fear of making mistakes, failing or taking risks; too much need for security, order and structure; preference for judging rather than generating ideas; impatience, which denies the chance to sleep on it or let ideas gestate sufficiently; and others. A manager who chooses to not try out using a new way of doing something may have an emotional block to the concept. Using different management approaches in an organization defies the traditional structure and certainly involves some risks. More will be said on this in Chapter Six.

> *"The pure and simple truth is rarely pure and never simple."* – Oscar Wilde

Perceptual Blocks. Many of these exist, including seeing what we expect to see, not being able to view things differently, etc. These blocks prevent the person from clearly perceiving either the problem itself or the information which is necessary to solve the problem. Too many people spend inadequate time defining the problem, in order to get on with the "important" part of solving it. This is a foolish tendency. The manager who has decided that the maintenance department is inept may be blinded to the real problem of equipment that is beyond repair.

Cultural Blocks. Taboos. Traditions. Excessive belief in logic, reason, numbers. Distrust of fantasy, intuition, and different drummers. In short, behaving the way

we're "supposed to" is conforming, not creative. As will be discussed in Chapter Six, organizations themselves have a culture. While conformity may be essential to a manager's acceptance by peers and superiors, it may also inhibit the implementation of needed changes.

Environmental Blocks. Distractions such as the telephone, e-mails and chatty colleagues. Lack of cooperation from co-workers. Autocratic bosses. Bureaucracy. Things in the workplace which keep you from being creative. Work environments are filled with environmental blocks. No single technique works to overcome these, but good time management techniques can sometimes reduce them.

Intellectual Blocks. These keep you from understanding concepts necessary to work on the problem. If you don't have the experience, academic training or mental abilities sophisticated enough to understand and deal with the issues surrounding the problem or decision, it's difficult to be creative. It could also be that you're locked into a bad approach. Managers who have been promoted from the ranks of workers often find themselves falling behind technologically, especially in fast changing fields. Their subordinates may understand new and advanced techniques which would work, but the manager might resist these fearing loss of control.

Expressive Blocks. Inadequate language skill to express and record ideas in a manner which can be understood by others. This could also apply to using the wrong or inappropriate medium to express concepts, such as trying to express a visual idea orally or a mathematical idea in visual terms. In today's more diverse workplaces, managers may find themselves with subordinates and peers who — literally — speak different languages. It takes so much energy for routine communications in these environments that creativity may be reduced.

Overcoming the Barriers to Creativity

Some of these blocks suggest their own remedies, if, in fact, they can be remedied. Certain people can not overcome these barriers; others do so only at great effort over time.

Generally, there are four fronts on which we must attack the barriers to creativity.

Overcoming Conceptual Barriers to Creativity according to Robert H. Vaughn

---

Change the CLIMATE of the organization.
Change the ATTITUTE of the individuals.
Work on DEVELOPING SKILLS.
Learn and use CREATIVITY TOOLS.

---

1. Change the Climate of the organization

Much of the reason we aren't creative is that the organizational or personal climate for encouraging or accepting creativity is bad. We may be afraid of making mistakes, or the job loss or personal embarrassment which results from those mistakes.

How much an individual can personally do to change the climate depends in part on where he or she is within the organization's hierarchy and with their own leadership skills. Someone who runs the organization (or a portion of it), probably can have a big influence on the climate. A person who is part of an employee group such as a Self-Managed Work Team (or participative management teams by whatever name), is probably in an organization open to the idea of change. It will be more difficult for the drones to effect any changes in organizational climate. More on organizational climate will be covered in Chapter Six.

2. Change the Attitude of the individuals

People vary in their personal thirst for creativity. Adams' list probably helps make the reasons more obvious. They come, at least in part, from an individual's early experiences in trying to be creative. If they were successful and accepted, a person probably has more willingness to continue to try later in life. If not, a person will probably be more comfortable to stay structured.

Resistance to creativity is normally an *attitude*, not a *value*. This means it can be changed with appropriate motivation. (Values can't

> *"Faced with the choice between changing one's mind and proving that there's no need to do so, almost everybody gets busy on the proof."*
>
> – John Kenneth Galbraith

change without what Morris Massey calls "a significant emotional experience." These would be such things as a brush with death or the like. Attitudes, fortunately, change more easily.)

Necessity is frequently the mother of invention. Yet, it is not enough to simply put someone into a situation requiring creativity, and expect them to be creative. That's akin to simply throwing someone into the water to teach them to swim. The blocks Adams lists develop over a long period of time. Getting rid of them requires you to do two things:

- *Consciously identify the barriers which interfere with your own creativity.* This bringing to the conscious level allows people to analyze the barriers which operate for them. Adams' categories provide a good framework for the identification and analysis.

- *Decide to allow yourself the freedom to be creative and to get into situations where you can begin to experiment with new ideas.* Practice in being creative can help. See the suggestions in "skill development" below.

For example, one possible way to identify and analyze your own creativity barriers include trying some brain teasers, puzzles, word games, or the like. After each failure, ask yourself what got in the way of originally solving it? Also, you might find it interesting and helpful to keep a record of things which kept you from being creative.

It's not enough to just overcome the barriers for that particular problem. You must understand the process you used and how it can be applied to the next situation. Otherwise, you've learned only for the one event, now past.

3. Work on Developing Skills

Remember that our purpose for encouraging creativity is pragmatic: We want to come up with a good, usable list of options from which to proceed to evaluate and solve problems or make decisions which create effective management plans and controls.

Below is a partial list of some things which can make a person more creative. This book, of course, does not advocate nor discuss all of the options listed. We'll limit ourselves to the legal and safer ones. We'll describe these one by one.

Some Things Which *Might* Enhance Individual Creativity

Practice	Necessity
Threats	Adversity
Competition	Lack of threats
Hallucinogens	Getting enough sleep
Using teams or groups	

– and –

Knowing some tools and tricks to overcome the creativity barriers.

Practice. This requires looking at old things in new ways. It requires putting yourself into situations where there's no clear response. Sometimes this can be as simple as deciding to take a new route to work. It may also take the form of joining a new group, trying a new restaurant, or going to an old restaurant but sitting somewhere different and ordering a different meal; visiting an art gallery or a science museum; or taking a class in creativity. Working on puzzles or games also can stimulate some creativity, as can debating issues with other people. The point is that it doesn't require a major change in lifestyle; simply a commitment to try to become more versatile in how you approach things.

> *"If you have always done it that way, it is probably wrong."* – Charles Kettering

Competition. For some people, competition is the extra motivation which spurs them to open up their own resources more effectively. It could be in the traditional sports sense of baseball or diving or skiing, or in chess or poker. It could also be in artistic ways such as writing or photography contests. It could be in your business career, working to make sure you're the one who gets the desired promotion. It could be in selling your company's product lines. It could be in the area of personal relationships to win the girl or guy of your dreams or to settle the argument that, "Mom always liked you best."

Mental Preparation. When we make our annual New Year's Resolution to shape up our physical condition, we are faced with the warnings from most of the medical profession: Get a check up, have a plan for your exercise program, get plenty of rest, eat healthy food, and be sure to "warm up" before undertaking strenuous exercise. Much of that same advice applies to developing our mental capacities. For example, when you're over-tired or hungry, it's hard to think at all, let alone be more creative. Pacing ourselves, proper rest and eating habits, and so on, will help our creativity.

As mentioned before, trying some brain teasers or puzzles and keeping track of the barriers you found hindering you may be useful. Part of mental preparation is keeping in practice and knowing what barriers you've encountered before so you can avoid them.

Our brains are marvelous, and humans are among the very few species which actively pursue creativity. But some of the biggest gains in civilization came from humans learning to use tools to extend their own physical and mental capabilities. That's where this book is heading. First, why is creativity important, then what are some tools we can use to enhance our creativity?

Using Teams or Groups. This is covered more in Chapter Six. Groups, in fact, are required in order to use some of the tools presented in the final four chapters.

Other items in the list. These are either self-explanatory, or need to be covered in an Organizational Behavior, Psychology, or Drug Abuse class.

4. Learning and Using Creativity Tools

Most people today don't attempt to build a house by hand. A mud hut or lean-to shelter would be the best that might be accomplished. Having a saw, hammer, nails and other tools will make it much easier to build a far superior house.

A wide variety of creativity tools has been developed which can help us overcome Adams' barriers. These include many which are widely understood and used, such as Brainstorming. Other "tools" are so common place that most people don't even consider them to be creativity aids. Using checklists and catalogs, for example, are excellent ways to come up with options which might never have been developed or considered without them.

It may seem strange that using a tool can help to *structure* creativity. That sounds paradoxical, yet it's true. Chapter Nine covers some of these tools which can aid your creativity by structuring how you approach the process.

The Importance of Creativity in Management

There are those persons who claim the phrase "creative management" is oxymoronic. Sarcasm aside, management <u>needs</u> to be creative — at least now and then.

Planning can't occur without some creativity. Problem solving can't either, unless it's a very simple problem. Decision making and control also need creativity. The previous chapter showed where creativity fits into decision making and problem solving. The table below shows how it fits into planning and control.

Note that all of these management functions also need the deductive or analytical stages, too. The analytical steps will be covered in the next chapter.

Planning Steps	Type of Tool	Control Steps	Type of Tool
Establish your goals	Creative	Establish standards	Creative
Define your limits	Inductive	Measure performance	Physical & Conceptual
Determine options	Inductive/Creative	Compare & Evaluate	Inductive (Creative) & Deductive
Evaluate options	Deductive	Correct Deviations	Sometimes Creative & sometimes Deductive
Choose the best	Deductive		
Implement/Recycle	Mixed		

Creativity Tools

These come in a variety of forms. Some can be used by an individual. Some require group interaction. Some focus on certain types of problems or decisions, while others are generic and seem to be applicable to nearly any issue.

Chapter Nine provides an introduction to some of the more popular creativity tools. You may wish to read that chapter following this one, or you may proceed with the narrative and theory portion first by just continuing on to Chapter Five. You will have heard of and used some of the creativity tools in Chapter Nine before. Some are so intuitive that you may have used them and never even thought about it being a tool for creativity.

When you are faced with a problem to solve or decision to make using one of these tools, you are encouraged to carefully follow the steps suggested in the tool chapters (8-11). As mentioned before, it may sound contradictory to suggest that being structured can make you more creative. It's really not, though, since we know that structure and discipline are necessary to excel at most human endeavors. Simply put, having a tool and knowing how to use it can make the task easier.

Summary

A wide variety of things can keep us from being creative, and many of these are deeply ingrained from our culture and our earliest childhood experiences. J.L. Adams categorizes these for us into: Emotional, Perceptual, Cultural, Environmental, Intellectual and Expressive Blocks. Understanding and analyzing which of these influence your personal creativity behavior is a first step to overcoming them.

Beyond that, becoming more creative can be aided by changes in the organizational climates in which we work, changing our own attitudes, specifically working at developing our creative skills, and learning a variety of tools which can help us enhance our creativity. Amazingly enough, many of these tools use a specific structured process which can be learned. Some of these tools are presented and explained in the next chapter.

Study Questions

1. What are the barriers to creativity, according to J. L. Adams?
2. What's the difference between a value and an attitude, as they relate to change?
3. Name some things an individual can do to increase their creativity.

4. True or false: We can enhance our creativity by using structured tools.
5. Which of the steps in planning are creative? Which of the steps in control are?

Exercises

Find some brain teasers and analyze which of Adams' blocks are involved. Here are a few to get you started:

- In the following line of letters, cross out six letters so that the remaining letters, without altering their sequence, will spell a familiar English word.

B S A I N X L E A T N T E A R S

- Complete the following equations by choosing the appropriate words represented by the letters. For example, 16 = O. in a P. would be "ounces - pound."

26 = L. of the A.	1001 = A. N.	3 = B.M. (S.H.T.R.)
1 = W. on a U.	7 = W. of the A. W.	13 = S. on the A. F.
11 = P. on a F. T.	12 = S. of the Z.	18 = H. on a G. C.

- How quickly can you find out what is so unusual about this paragraph? It looks so ordinary that you would think that nothing at all is wrong with it, and — in fact — nothing is. But it is unusual. Why? If you study it and think about it, you may find out, but I am not going to assist you in any way. You must do it without coaching. No doubt, if you work at it for long, it will dawn on you. Who knows? Par is about half an hour.

Make a list of organizational barriers to creativity at an organization where you have worked. Which techniques might be used to reduce these barriers?

Note: Answers to these exercises are on the computer support disk which comes with the book.

CHAPTER 5

Gathering Information and Analyzing Possibilities

"Life is full of choices.... and sometimes all of them are yucky!"

– Joanne Lee

Chapter Objectives:

This chapter is designed to enable the reader to ....
- Identify significant sources of data for analysis of options.
- Determine the value of obtaining additional information.
- Explain and use Pareto analysis.
- Define "risk" in terms of decision making and problem solving.
- Explain how to collect and stratify data for effective use in decision making and problem solving.
- Explain and use elementary principles of probability theory.
- Explain how to determine the relationship between data sets.

B y using the creativity approaches suggested in Chapter Four (and perhaps the tools in Chapter Nine), you now have the ability to develop good lists of options. This knowledge and skill are necessary, but not yet sufficient in the processes of decision making and problem solving. You can get part way through, but there's more to be done.

What if all of the options you've developed sound pretty good, but you still have to make a choice of just one or two? Which option is best? Sometimes, that's an easy question, and sometimes it's not. If you're making a simple decision — the red jacket or the blue one — the outcome is really not that important. You'll go with your gut feeling and move on.

On the other hand, if you're considering moving your production plant to another site or buying a house or making some other decision which has a major impact in terms of money or other criteria, as we discussed in Chapter Four, you'll need to be particularly careful to make the right choice.

This chapter will cover a variety of different points which should be considered as you begin to evaluate which option to choose. First, we'll cover some major sources of data to help make your decision. Frequently, so much information is available that it can be overwhelming and get in the way of effective decision making. To deal with this, we'll cover ideas on determining how much information you need, how to prioritize it, and how to collect and organize it in the most efficient manner. Finally, we'll cover some information on how to collect and deal with sample data. This last part isn't necessary for all decision making analysis, but it does have a wide variety of applications. We'll begin with a look at where to find information on your options.

Too much information can be as much a problem as too little information.

Possible Sources of Information for the Analysis

You will usually be aware of the obvious sources of information about your options. The sources are often unique to the nature of the problem you're trying to solve. This information may be internal to your organization, or you may need to go to sources outside your department, company or industry.

All information comes from some form of simple or complex "research." In some cases, you may need to create and collect **primary data**. Primary data comes from basic experimentation. We have to test things out and see how they actually perform. Quality control testing is an example of collecting primary data. So is designing and conducting a survey.

Much of our decision making information, however, comes from **secondary data**, which means data collected by someone else, often for some other purpose, but which is usable for our decision. Examples of secondary data include information from catalogs, census reports, and so on.

Let's go back to the earlier example of making a decision about which car to buy. We would probably gather data about this through both techniques. We would look up information in various publications such as *Consumer Reports* or *Car and Driver*, but we'd probably also visit a showroom for a test drive and to get other sensory perceptions. Obviously what sources we use for the data depends on what we need to know, what's available in secondary sources, how easily and inexpensively we can get that, and a number of other factors.

What do we really need to know in order to make a decision? Generally we will want to collect only data that's going to be of use to us. On most decisions, there will be many pieces of information which we could collect.

For example, if we're ready to buy the car, we could check hundreds of things about each option, including fuel tank capacity, length of the windshield wiper blades and many other obscure criteria. But why? We want to get enough information to make a good decision, but not so much as to overwhelm us or cloud the issue.

Experts tell us that one major reason for poor decisions is TOO MUCH data. This is particularly true since the advent of the computer. It's now possible to analyze information easily and report it quickly. However, it may still not be good or necessary information. (Reportedly, one of the major reasons U.S. defense intelligence people missed some of the recent developments with Korea was "data pollution." They had too much information.) We must sort out what's really important.

Secondary data is nearly always cheaper if it is available in a form which applies to our decision. If we're buying a new piece of equipment, secondary data sources would include promotional literature from the manufacturer. We might expect this to be biased,

55

and if we're looking at several pieces of equipment, the promotional information from each might not allow us to make a clear comparison with others. Perhaps we can find some objective comparison published in a periodical. *Consumer Reports* is a well known publication which does this, but it only covers merchandise of interest to the general public. What if we want to compare commercial or industrial equipment options?

Once upon a time, finding information in periodicals meant going to the library where the periodical was located and either thumbing through the tables of contents of issues on file or finding the annual index. Today, the search of these references is largely done through hundreds of commercially available data bases and websites which allow Internet access to quickly help find information on any topic imaginable. Detailing use of these is beyond the scope of this book. The only caution to be issued here is that, while the Internet has become an amazing resource for research, it requires skill to separate the fact from the fiction. The typical Internet search is confounded by two issues: volume and credibility. Enter a search term or question in most of the search engines (Google, Yahoo!, Ask.com, and hundreds more), and a typical inquiry may come back with thousands of references. Some may be very credible, and some are posted by the ten-year old down the street. It's not enough to find information on the internet; you must also be able to verify its accuracy. Most libraries can help you learn how to reach appropriate resources and minimize the volume issue through appropriate searching techniques. Again, this is a complex subject and way beyond the scope of this particular book.

Pareto Analysis

One way of evaluating the importance of a piece of data in making a decision is to consider a concept called Pareto Analysis. While it's named after a real person (Vilfredo Pareto, a nineteenth century Italian mathematician and philosopher), it's not really a statistical analysis. The concept is also sometimes called "the 80-20 Rule", and relates to "A-B-C Analysis" in inventory planning and control. In general, it suggests that typically:

"About 80% of the activity comes in 20% of the participants, while
About 20% of the activity comes from 80% of the participants."

To demonstrate this, consider the telephone calls you received last year. 80% of them may have come from 20% of your callers. The other 20% of the calls came from the 80% of the people who called you once or twice during the year. Is this precisely accurate? Of course not, but the generalized concept is probably true. How do you spend time in the various rooms in your home? Probably a few rooms make up most of your time; certain rooms you seldom visit. If you run a grocery store, a large part of your sales comes from a small part of your stock. Milk & Bread may make up less than 1% of your stock in units or price, but 7 or 8% your sales volume.

Pareto "analysis", then, is looking at a collection of data and striving to **distinguish the "significant few" from the "trivial many."** In this way, you are able to prioritize and focus on areas where your efforts can be most rewarded.

For example, if you change phone numbers, notifying just a few key people will mean that most of your calls will be received correctly. If you don't have time to clean the whole house, cleaning only the most used rooms will give you the greatest peace of mind. If you're operating the convenience store, it will matter less if you run out of canned mushrooms than if you run out of 2% milk, so you'll focus on key needs as you make orders from suppliers.

Pareto analysis asks you separate the "trivial many" from the "significant few."

To use this concept, simply make a list of the data you <u>could</u> collect, then put it into a list in the order of its importance to your decision. You'll certainly collect the first item or two on the list. As you go down to each subsequent piece of information you might collect, ask yourself how valuable that information is to your decision and how much it will take to collect it. If you predict that it will take a lot of time or cost a lot of money, ask yourself if the additional information will really be that helpful in making a good decision? Will it be cost-effective or not? If not, don't collect the information.

How Much Information Do You Need?

We discussed earlier that there's probably no need to look at every possible car you could buy before you make your choice. Part of the evaluation process is to decide "how much data is enough?"

Sometimes we can determine the exact number of available choices. When this happens, we have a **known population** or **known universe**. Most choices we make come from finite, rather than infinite, populations, but some of them are still quite large.

In some decision making exercises, we narrow down the population by putting increasingly restrictive limits on our options until we reach a small enough number or narrow enough focus that we can deal with it. In other cases, we may have to remove limits in order to increase the potential choices we have available.

For example, when we're looking for a car to buy, we keep adding (or sometimes dropping) limits until we get to a reasonable number of cars available to consider. We probably start with price and style (sports model or minivan, etc.), then further limit the number available by deciding we'll only buy from certain dealers and we must have certain options such as automatic transmission, etc. The net effect is to reduce the number of available cars we'll really consider. When we get it to a manageable number, then we really begin to compare.

Sometimes, though, when we're gathering information for analysis, we can't add limits to the population. For example, if we're checking on quality control, we can't decide to check parts from only one machine. On the other hand, we can't check all parts from all machines, since that would be time consuming and expensive... and sometimes impossible. Did you hear about the company that went out of business because the boss demanded 100% inspection and testing of every ink jet cartridge it produced?

So when do we have enough information? The answer to this requires us to consider the amount of risk involved in the decision we must make. Understanding risk, however, first requires an elementary understanding of probability.

An Introduction to Probability Concepts

Knowing the population with which we're dealing allows us to predict the likelihood of certain things happening. Essentially, all gambling is based on this fact. Let's look at the **probability** (or "odds") of certain things happening when you gamble.

If you flip a fair coin (i.e., not a shaved, two headed, weighted or otherwise unfair coin), the odds of getting heads or tails are 50% each. It's likely that after 10,000 coin flips you'd have pretty close to 5,000 heads and 5,000 tails. Each time you flip it you have, regardless of past performance, an equal chance of getting a head or a tail.

If, by chance, you've flipped the coin nine times in a row and had nine tails, the chance of getting head next time is still only 50%. It seems logical to think that a head just has to come up, but even if you've had 99 heads in a row, you still have only a 50% chance of a head on the next flip. (Personally, though, with 99 in a row, I'd ask for a different coin. The odds of 99 in a row are 0.5 to the 99th power, or approximately 1 to 1578 followed by 27 zeros!)

The term **gambler's fallacy** applies to the belief that you must have a greater than 50% chance, under those circumstances, of getting a head. You don't. Gambler's fallacy is the belief that a series of unrelated events changes the odds of a future one. For example: If I've never drawn an inside straight, my odds of doing so are getting better (No); If Sheila has turned me down for a date ten times in a row, she'll eventually say yes (doubtful).

Let's move on to something more complicated than flipping a coin — namely, rolling dice.

If you roll a fair set of dice, there are only certain possible outcomes. You can come up with only numbers between two and twelve, inclusive. You can also predict the probability of each possible number coming up. If you look at all possible outcomes, there are 36 ways the dice can land.

To keep it clear, let's say we have a red and a blue die. We can then roll:

Red 1 / Blue 1	Red 1 / Blue 2	Red 1 / Blue 3	Red 1 / Blue 4	Red 1 / Blue 5	Red 1 / Blue 6
Red 2 / Blue 1	Red 2 / Blue 2	Red 2 / Blue 3	Red 2 / Blue 4	Red 2 / Blue 5	Red 2 / Blue 6
Red 3 / Blue 1	Red 3 / Blue 2	Red 3 / Blue 3	Red 3 / Blue 4	Red 3 / Blue 5	Red 3 / Blue 6
Red 4 / Blue 1	Red 4 / Blue 2	Red 4 / Blue 3	Red 4 / Blue 4	Red 4 / Blue 5	Red 4 / Blue 6
Red 5 / Blue 1	Red 5 / Blue 2	Red 5 / Blue 3	Red 5 / Blue 4	Red 5 / Blue 5	Red 5 / Blue 6
Red 6 / Blue 1	Red 6 / Blue 2	Red 6 / Blue 3	Red 6 / Blue 4	Red 6 / Blue 5	Red 6 / Blue 6

No other outcomes are possible. That's thirty six possible outcomes for our "population". Each has an equal chance of occurring.

How many of those combinations add up to Two? Only one: Red 1 /Blue 1. How many add up to three? Two: Red 1 / Blue 2 and Red 2 / Blue 1. If you carry out this analysis, you'll find that the odds of getting certain numbers on a roll of a pair of fair dice are as follows:

$$2 = 1/36 \text{ or } .028 \qquad\qquad 12 = 1/36 \text{ or } .028$$
$$3 = 2/36 \text{ or } .056 \qquad\qquad 11 = 2/36 \text{ or } .056$$
$$4 = 3/36 \text{ or } .083 \qquad\qquad 10 = 3/36 \text{ or } .083$$
$$5 = 4/36 \text{ or } .111 \qquad\qquad 9 = 4/36 \text{ or } .111$$
$$6 = 5/36 \text{ or } .139 \qquad\qquad 8 = 5/36 \text{ or } .139$$
$$7 = 6/36 \text{ or } .167$$

All of these add up to 1.000 or 100%, since you must get one of these numbers when you roll a pair of dice.

If you apply the same logic to a fair deck of poker cards (no jokers), you can also determine the probability of drawing certain cards. Assuming you know what's in a standard poker style deck, what are the odds of drawing an Ace? Four aces exist among the fifty two cards. Therefore, the chances are 4 out of 52 (or the odds are 1:12). The odds of getting a diamond? 13 out of 52 or 1:3. The odds of getting black card? 26 out of 52 or 1:1. The odds of getting the Queen of Hearts? Only one out of fifty-two cards is the queen of hearts, so the odds are 1:51.

Understanding the concept of probability can never, of course, tell you for sure what will happen. It does, however, give you information to help determine how much risk there is in some of the decisions you're making. See the appendix for further information and simple calculation techniques.

Risk in the Decision

You know from your personal experience that people vary in the amount of risk they will take. Again, we leave to the behaviorists the reasons behind the phenomenon of risk taking. We know that it is influenced by such things as personality, consequences of loss, benefits of gain, group pressure, and many other things, even including the way in which the risk is stated.

A graphical depiction of these differences is shown below, and explained in the following paragraph.

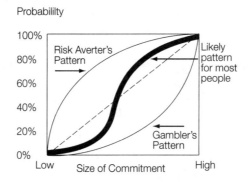

Sample Preference Curves

Preference theory (also called utility theory) is based on the notion that individual attitudes toward risk will vary. Some people, called **risk averters** will take lower risks than indicated by the probabilities, while others, called **gamblers** will take greater risks. It might seem logical that if a person was given a decision with a 75% probability of one choice being the correct one, it would be chosen. But this is not necessarily true, since there is a 25% chance of the decision being wrong. Some people will avoid even small risks, especially if the penalty for being wrong is severe.

As shown by the darker line in the graph, most people will take some risk when the commitment is low, but will become conservative as the stakes increase. You might be willing to bet $1.00 at 10:1 odds to win a payoff of $5.00. But if it's a $100.00 bet for $500.00 at the same odds, most of us would be more reluctant. It's not the *odds* (they're both ten to one against you) or the *payoff* (both five to one if you win), but the *size of the commitment*. We can afford to lose the one dollar, but not the one hundred dollars.

Probability (shown on the vertical axis of the chart) is an important concept in the analysis of risk. We all hear weather reports saying that the "probability of rain is 60%." What does this really mean? Does it mean that there are five meteorologists in the office and three think it will rain? Maybe.

The higher the risk, then, the more information we will probably want to collect to help insure that our decision is correct.

Formulas exist in management science which can help determine the value of additional information. A simplified way of dealing with it is to ask, "What will the additional information cost (in time, money or other resources)?" And, "What is the risk of deciding without it? Sometimes this can be quantified (an example will be given in a later chapter), but often it can't. It becomes a judgment call. If the risk is low and the additional information expensive or time consuming to obtain, odds are that it won't be worth it. If the risk is high and the additional information can be obtained easily, then go ahead and get it. More points to consider about this question are included in the appendix.

All this is further complicated by a concept called "framing" which will be discussed in Chapter Six. Framing may cause a person to make different choices, even when the probability is the same.

Organizing the Data for Analysis

Once you have determined which data is important to have, you must collect and organize it. The organization is essential. For example, it is usually necessary to stratify data into proper groupings. **Stratification** means to divide or sort into two or more meaningful groups which can be examined separately.

If you don't do this, you end up like the audience when a sportscaster came in slightly under the influence one night. He reported the following to his confused audience: "And now, ladies and gentlemen, here are tonight's scores: 37 to 41, 66 to 12, 39 to 22, 18 to 44, and, in a big upset, 52 to 33!" You know *something*, but it's not all that clear or useful. The names of the teams and which sport he's discussing would be helpful to understanding the concept and relevance of his points..

Stratification makes irregularities or relationships more readily stand out. It is, therefore, an essential aid to problem solving and decision making.

The Steps in Stratifying Include:

1. Plan how the data should be divided for easiest handling.

2. Carefully sort the different data into the proper categories.

3. Separate those categories of data which are needed for your problem solving process or decision making from those which are not. (Collect data that can't be used by you or your department only if it is needed by others.)

4. Collect the data on a stratified basis from the beginning, when possible. Avoid random samples which are mixed.

For example, if you're gathering data to be used for quality control, and you have several possible sources of poor quality, make certain you can trace any problem to its cause. This may mean collecting data separately from each machine or each worker or each supplier. This will reduce difficulties during the problem solving stage.

For a small population of options, you may want to get information on all of them. For example, if you're trying to decide which among five computer systems to buy, you should get details on each.

But let's say you want information on how your customers would react to a change in your product design. If you only have a few customers, you might ask them all. But if you have thousands of customers, you'll never get all their opinions. Or if you do, it'll be very expensive and time consuming.

For a large population, you can get reasonably reliable information by selecting a small, appropriate sample amount of that population to examine. **Sampling** is widely accepted in our culture, in things such as TV Arbitron ratings or political polls or free samples of food given in grocery stores.

An Introduction to Sampling Concepts

This summary is not intended to provide a comprehensive treatment of the subject of sampling. Like the rest of the book, it is written for the layman - manager who will use it as a tool for gathering data to help with problem solving or decision making.

How many samples you need is determined by the nature of what you're sampling. In the grocery store, you may only need one taste of Harry's Horribly Hot Jalapeno Dip to decide whether or not you want to buy it. On the other hand, Harry probably needs to sample quite a few cans of his production to insure that the quality is staying where he wants it. He also needs to sample a number of customers to see if the recipe needs to be changed. He probably should not change it based on just one person's opinion.

Sometimes the information you get by sampling is just a "yes" or "no". Sampling responses could also take the form of a variety of options (e.g., red, orange, yellow, green, blue or paisley). If you're trying to determine the most popular dress colors this year, you can do that by sampling. You simply need to set up a category for each color, and collect information in some reasonable fashion (pun attempted; can't win them all).

For sampling to be useful, the sample must truly represent the entire population from which it is taken. For example, a poll to determine political attitudes of the country could not be conducted only in Boston or only in San Diego. To insure the representativeness of a sample, you must first know something about the population.

Populations which are truly homogeneous can be sampled in any manner. Probably very few truly homogeneous populations exist, but there are many in which the differences are not significant or not related to the variable being measured. **Random Samples** can be taken at any time, any place, in any order. All that's necessary is to get a sufficient quantity of samples.

In many cases, however, **Stratified Samples** are necessary. To stratify means to insure that there is a representative mix of the population within the sample. Let's use an example. If you're doing work sampling (see Tool # 20), you need to sample across all time periods and job categories. If you sampled only mornings or only materials handlers, your information would only be usable for that group at that time.

Common bases for stratification include:

- *Time* – Commonly, an equal number of samples is taken each hour of operation.
- *Location* – All locations of operation should be appropriately represented in the sample.
- *Machine* – Products made on various machines need to be included in the sample to insure overall accuracy.
- *Worker* – Work done by each worker needs to be included in the sample.
- *Demographic Data* – Public opinion surveys need to include representative mixes of various ages, races, employment categories, income levels, etc.
- *Et Cetra* – Any categories which could potentially provide different data than the rest of the sample need to be proportionately included.

You can determine through statistical means how accurately and with what level of confidence a sample represents its population. An easy to remember number which is a standard in the sampling business is **1111**. That's the largest number of samples you'll ever need to take of a population to be 98% certain that your sample is within plus or minus 3% of the actual population. Depending on what you're sampling, it can require dramatically fewer samples than that. A quick reference table and the basic formulas are shown in the appendix.

Further information about relationships between groups of data can be determined by testing the correlation of these groups with each other. If two sets of data have a high degree of correlation, you probably only need to collect one. For example, if you wish to know how many cows and horses are in a field, you need only count the heads of each type of animal. There's no need to also count feet, since you can be relatively sure that each head will represent four feet with a very high degree of correlation (except around the Chernobyl area in Russia).

An Introduction to Data Correlation

Correlation is an indicator of how much relationship there is between two sets of data. When two sets of data which have a high correlation are plotted on a graph, it will be easy to draw a single straight or smooth curved line which would pass fairly close to all the points. While there are, of course, statistical means for determining how good the correlation is (see the appendix), a visual check may be all that's needed to determine whether the data is one set is related at all to the data from the other. Samples are shown below.

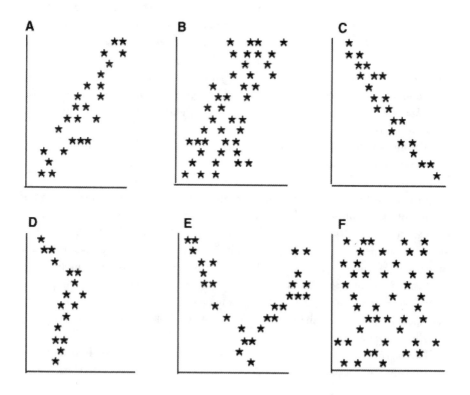

For example, if we were to gather information from a group of people and plot their height on the vertical scale and their weight on the horizontal scale, which of the preceeding patterns would you expect to emerge? How about if we plotted the selling price of a bag of popcorn at a movie on the vertical and the number of bags sold on the horizontal scale? Typically, of course, the height to weight ratios would be positive, but loose, as (B) would indicate. The price to purchase relationship for popcorn probably would be negative (C), meaning the higher the price, the less would be sold.

A positive relationship means that as one number increases, the other will also. A negative relationship means that as one increases, the other decreases. "Tightness" and "looseness" have to do with how precise the relationship is — or how close to a straight line the plotted points would make. In the example plots, the numbers plotted on D and E probably have some complex mathematical relationship to each other, but it's clearly not a straight line. The two sets of numbers plotted on F appear to have no relationship to each other.

A final word of caution: Even if your data looks like (A) or (C), there is no guarantee that correlation exists. If it looks like (F), you can probably be fairly sure that no correlation exists, but — again — not positive. Further information on these concepts may be obtained from a statistics course or textbook.

Summary

This chapter has detailed a number of different factors a manager must consider as the options are evaluated during the decision making and problem solving process.

Possible sources of data are discussed in general terms. The decision maker or problem solver must consider how much information is needed. Pareto analysis was suggested as one technique which might help determine that. Gathering the data through sampling was covered next, emphasizing the need to plan what is needed and collect it in way which will allow efficient use for analysis. Once the data has been gathered, it must be organized effectively.

Finally, unless there's a clear winner among the options, we need to understand the concepts of risk and probability to determine whether we need to collect more data, or whether we can accept the risk of error at this stage of the process. The actual decision is then made using tools described later in this book.

Data sources, risk, Pareto analysis, stratification, probability and correlation are important concepts in preparing the information you collect for analysis. However, these concepts will not answer which of the options is best. They _will_ provide a structure to the information to _help_ your decision making.

The tools described in Chapters Ten and Eleven can be used for this analysis and comparison of options. You may want to move on to those chapters now, or you may wish to continue with Chapters Six and Seven and complete the theory part of the book.

Study Questions:

1. Define primary and secondary data.
2. What is the most practical way to use Pareto analysis, according to this chapter?
3. Does an honest deck of cards represent a known or an unknown universe?
4. What influences the amount of risk an individual will take?
5. Define stratification.
6. If there is a mathematical relationship between two sets of numbers, they are said to be ____?
7. Why is sampling a good idea in collection of information?

Exercises:

Do ten sit-ups, run in place for fifteen minutes, and then do twenty push-ups.

List potential sources of primary and secondary information for a decision whether to move your company offices to another nearby city.

Collect information on two factors you would expect to be correlated, then plot the results and observe the chart. Were you correct in your assumption? Are you sure?

6

Other Considerations in Decision Making

"It is much more pleasant to make the decision than to justify it."

– Malcolm Forbes

Chapter Objectives:

This chapter is designed to enable the reader to ....

- Describe the advantages and disadvantages of teams (or groups) in managerial problem solving and decision making.
- Describe the basic requirements for and stages of evolution of a group.
- Describe the effect of organizational climate on decision making and problem solving.
- Describe the effect of technology on decision making and problem solving.
- Describe the effect of organization structure on decision making and problem solving.
- Describe the psychological effects of decision framing on the resulting decision.
- Explain the role of critical thinking in decision making and problem solving.
- Define the differences between theory and reality in decision making and problem solving.

Each of the headings in this chapter has been the subject of complete books and much research. Obviously, we're just going to scratch the surface as we discuss them. Yet, each may have a significant impact on the decision making process as it has been discussed so far in this text.

The word "team" has been used frequently in this book as well as much of the current literature. "Team" is the current word of choice when discussing the group. Both organizational culture and group dynamics influence how effectively a team can function. Some of the tools to be discussed in Chapters 8–11 require a group to operate (Brainstorming, for example). Technology, another chapter topic, will influence both how and how fast decision making will happen in your organization. Framing has to do with our personal understanding and use of probabilities. The final topic to be addressed in this chapter, Theory vs. Reality, attempts to put into perspective all of the structured processes presented in the preceding five chapters.

Group Dynamics

Groups can be strange creatures. You hear conflicting stories. Some people say that two heads are better than one, and that groups create a **synergy** in which creativity and quality can flourish. Others cite the opposite, but commonly heard ideas that: "A camel is a racehorse put together by a committee;" "The best committee has three people, two of whom are always absent;" "No one ever erected a memorial to a committee."

Are groups good or bad? The answer is, "Yes!" To explain slightly more than that (just in case your boss won't take "yes" for an answer), we're going to look briefly at how groups develop and how they make decisions. For further study, refer to a textbook or other resource on organizational behavior, sociology, or a related field.

Group Development

Groups are essential for certain things. They are usually formed to do things that can't be done by one person. The development of any group (team, club, committee, or whatever) will go through some predictable stages. These have been defined as *forming, storming, norming and performing*. This description comes from Bruce W. Tuckman, who obviously has a serious hang-up on gerunds. Nevertheless, it is a cute memory jogger and reasonably accurate.

Forming is when the group first begins to exist. People generally like to be with other people. Maslow, Alderfer, McClelland, and virtually any motivation theorist will cite socialization as a strong need of most humans and many lower species including fish, ants and college fraternities. Groups usually form around some purpose: people were assigned (as in a committee), people have some common interest (as in a church or a company softball league), people were hired to do a job for an organization (as in the print shop), or people just meet by happenstance and try to make themselves comfortable (as in the typical wedding reception).

What happens when you meet someone at a wedding reception? Usually the conversation begins with either very idle chatter ("Hot today, isn't it?") or some kind of question designed to find out what the two people have in common ("Are you a friend of the bride or groom?" or "What town do you live in?"). If commonalties emerge, the conversation may flourish and a "group" of sorts develops. If no reason to continue the conversation (and therefore the beginnings of a group) becomes apparent, the individuals drift on and repeat the process with others. Forming, then, is the stage of group development where people get to know the others and begin to establish the commonalties.

> "Football combines two of the worst elements of American society: violence and committee meetings." – George Will

Sometimes the original basis for the group comes from a job or assigned task, as when a college professor assigns group projects or a boss assigns people to shifts. Many times, a group simply emerges from some common interest, such as model railroading or riding motorcycles or saving the whales. (I knew a guy who had the whole collection.)

Storming is the period of confusion inherent to any effort involving new relationships among people. We learn what each others' skills and attitudes are, and we try to get organized. Who's leading, who's following, how can we divide the tasks, what sub-groups exist or will emerge, and all of the various sociopolitical aspects of group membership and direction must be determined. If goals have not been designated by this point, options are considered and argued over.

Norming is when the group has achieved a certain equilibrium or oneness, and begins to establish rules for itself and its members. A cohesiveness among members develops, and norms (norms are unwritten rules) begin to govern behavior. A pecking order has emerged, and the group is now becoming ready to turn outward and deal with the tasks and goals it seeks to accomplish.

Performing is the mature stage of the group when it can operate with the positive benefits that people seek to achieve when groups are formed.

Some of the predictable things which happen when groups form include:

- Groups will evolve, often far beyond the original reason for their formation.
- Leaders will emerge to serve the group at different stages.
- Rules (norms) will evolve which will allow the group to continue to exist. — These may be either good or bad for the larger organization.
- Finally, a level of cohesiveness will develop which is comfortable to the members.

Managers and group leaders typically should encourage norms and cohesiveness which support the larger organization, and discourage those which cause divisiveness and excessive conflict. For example, managers may want work teams which can make their own decisions and they would encourage a norm of group autonomy. On the other hand, if a group norm of "minimal effort on the job" or of "not dealing with paperwork" develops, management will probably try to change these norms.

Group Decision Making

Some predictable things also happen as groups begin to make decisions.

- Groups tend to make decisions more slowly than do individuals.
- Groups tend to make decisions which are more extreme (exaggerating conservative or radical tendencies) than those made by the individual members.
- Groups are often subject to weak decisions supported by a minority of the members.
- Groups may have to compromise, making their decisions less effective than desired.

Managers need to be aware of these concerns. For example, if a quick decision is needed, a group decision should be avoided when possible. But there are real advantages to group decision making.

Situations where a group decision may be better include when:
- Input is needed from different perspectives (for example from sales and finance and production).
- Support for the decision needs to be developed (members of the team can take more detail and credibility back to their constituencies).
- Individuals need to feel involved.
- Creativity would be helpful (a wide range of alternatives is needed).
- Limited precedents exist for the problem to be solved or decision needed.
- Any of a variety of options would be acceptable to management.

Group decisions may be undesirable in other situations, such as when:
- Time is a critical factor.
- The group does not have expertise in the issue.
- Group norms don't agree with management objectives in the organization.
- The group is significantly dominated by one or a few members.
- And for other reasons suggested by the hazards mentioned previously.

Certain types of decisions — regardless of participative management theory — are very seldom delegated to a group. Groups don't do well in matters of resolving conflict, discipline (except as a jury), counseling, motivational problems, and so on. Some tasks in most organizations are made the sole responsibility of specific managers, and therefore can't be delegated to a group. The group may, however, act as an advisory body or sounding board in the decision making process by the manager.

If you were to take an organizational behavior class (or have done so), you'd probably spend at least a third of the course time covering the information summarized in the "Group Dynamics" heading. Again, this is a very superficial summary, but is included because the topics are truly relevant to the subjects of decision making and problem solving in management.

Organizational Structure, Climate and Culture

The structure of an organization can significantly influence its decision making processes. As in the previous paragraphs, we're going to be extremely abbreviated in the coverage of these topics. One obvious organizational structure factor in this regard is **centralization**, which, by definition, is a description of where in the organization decision making power resides. In a centralized organization, decisions are made at one place — usually at the top of the hierarchy. In a decentralized organization, decision making responsibility is dispersed various places within the organization, with decisions typically pushed as low in the hierarchy as practical. Of course many of the newer forms of organization are not hierarchical, but they are still subject to the concept of centralization.

Another factor influencing problem solving and decision making would be the **span of management** in a company. The wider the span of management, the more workers each supervisor must deal with. The **complexity** of an organization also influences the decision making process, as does the structure which is used (for example traditional, matrix or other forms).

Sometimes organizational structure is influenced or determined by external factors. For example, companies which deal with the Nuclear Regulatory Commission may be required to have Quality Assurance report directly to the chief executive, rather than to the manager of operations. Certainly external factors such as government regulation, the competitive environment (for example, does the company operate in an oligopoly or nearly pure competition? etc.), and many other things may have a significance in the decision making. For additional information on these subjects, see a more complete Principles of Management textbook.

Organizational Climate is generally defined as incumbent perceptions of what is important in the organization: policies, practices, procedures, reward, support and expectations. Organizational Culture is a little deeper: values, meanings and norms shared by organizational members make up the culture.

Climate was briefly covered in an earlier chapter in relation to creativity. Both the climate and culture in an organization will affect individual and group functioning by:

- encouraging or stifling creativity and risk,
- influencing the flow of information,
- supporting or discouraging decentralization of authority,
- advocating individuality or teamwork, and
- hundreds of other subtle and not-so-subtle ways.

Again, this topic is too broad to treat in depth in this book, and the reader is referred to other management or organizational behavior sources.

Technology

One obvious influence of technology on decision making is the availability of tools such as artificial intelligence, computer software, etc., within the organization. Even if the tools are available, the expertise to use them is also needed.

The faster technology changes, the more rapidly decisions will be needed and the more pressure comes with the decisions. So high technology organizations and their managers and teams will usually find higher levels of stress. There will also be more need for research to develop options (which are obsoleted and replaced quickly), and to make quick decisions, often with great levels of risk.

Also, higher technology makes more data available and increases the risk of information overload. One may find people dreaming of the good old days when chocolate and vanilla were those main choices. That's not likely to happen again, as pointed out by Barry Schwartz in his book, *The Paradox of Choice*.

What this all means is that higher technology organizations must become more familiar with the concepts presented in this book in order to maintain their competitiveness. Decision making and problem solving must be streamlined in the process, handled at the most efficient level of the organization, and leveraged with appropriate tools.

Decision Framing

We discussed the concepts of probability and risk in Chapter Five. One of the points that we didn't explain then was the idea of how our psychological impression of risk can be influenced by a concept called *framing*. Some of the early work on this phenomenon was done by Kahneman & Tversky in 1974.

What they found was that the way a problem is stated may significantly alter the level of risk which we assign to a situation. In oversimplified terms, this is the "glass half full" or "glass half empty" phenomenon. While both terms accurately describe a 50% filled beverage container, it shows that different people look at the same problem differently. In their studies, Kanneman & Teversky used college students as subjects in various risk taking exercises. As just one example, they found a substantial difference between groups in the number of students who said they would buy insurance if they were told there was an 80% chance that they *would not* be in an accident than if they were told there was a 20% chance that they *would* be in an accident. Obviously, the risk is the same, but simply stated from either a positive or negative perspective. The group which was given the negative perspective (20% chance you will be in an accident) was much more likely to purchase the theoretical insurance.

As you can imagine, this is a popular study in the marketing field. It deserves some significant attention in decision making and problem solving, as well. This leads us to the general concept of Critical Thinking.

Critical Thinking

The critical thinking movement is gaining in both education and business. If you read the accounts of the Challenger or Chernobyl or many other major business and scientific disasters, it's hard not to ask yourself whether these could have been prevented or reduced if only people had insisted on real answers rather than just following the rules. Some good case studies on this can be found in Paul C. Nutt's book, *Why Decisions Fail.*

The rapidly changing environment in most businesses often requires managers to make complex decisions without adequate time or resources to do the information gathering and analysis discussed in Chapter Five. They must rely on intuition, gut feelings, and personal background in the field, rather than hard facts that fit neatly into a decision matrix or break-even analysis (tools which will be discussed in upcoming chapters).

Acquisition of facts does not constitute knowledge.

The way in which managers internalize their training and automate their decision process skills may eventually — once they're comfortable in the field — begin to cause an over reliance on rules and precedents. This undercuts using the higher order thinking skills which are essential to effective management. Acquisition of facts does not constitute knowledge. For this reason, how a decision is made may be as important as the decision itself.

To avoid the trap of rote decision making rather than critical thinking, William Hisker suggests several key points:

- Managers must accept responsibility for their own learning and be active participants in it.
- Managers must know their area of specialty and how it interrelates to others in an organization.
- Open mindedness and fairness of thought require that managers accept that not all perspectives are based on observable facts.
- Managers must be aware of the processes you use to make decisions. In effect, you must think about your thinking. Their processes must be clear, precise and specific.
- Managers must be able to communicate effectively.
- Managers must be willing to synthesize, retrace, let things gestate, and innovate.
- Managers must also be open to the ideas of others, and be willing to integrate them into workable solutions.

Theory vs. Reality

What you've read in the first five chapters this book is the <u>theory</u> about decision making. What is the <u>reality</u>? The concept part of the book is nearly finished, after all.

The reality of decision making, as Kaplan and McCall point out, is nowhere near as neat. These four step, six step, nine step processes don't actually work that way. Reality is more ambiguous, more amorphous, more nebulous. "Problem solving/decision making techniques," they say, "are worth teaching, but a real effort must be made to point out the limited conditions under which they can be applied. A more practical approach to training managers in decision making is to accept that there is no 'quick fix'. The mixture of skills, knowledge and contacts underlying managerial actions must accumulate over time."

Why, then, have you labored through more than six dozen pages of "theory?" Alas, was it all in vain? Probably not.

Recall the discussion from the first chapter of learning letters before words and words and meaning before spelling and grammar. You need the basic building blocks to be able to approach a complex discipline. And management is a complex discipline. Further on, we described the advantages of a structure for decision making: confidence, known patterns, and so on.

Theory helps you to deal better with reality. Part of the purpose of this book has been to provide some theory. But the next part of the book is an attempt to provide you with some tools you can use as you face the reality of the decisions you must make as managers. Chapter Seven suggests techniques to get your decisions accepted, once they have been made.

Summary

This chapter has briefly covered a potpourri of issues related to decision making in organizations. Group development was described, listing some stages of development as well as facts about groups which management needs to consider. The pros and cons of using a group to make decisions were discussed. The influences of organizational structure, climate and culture and technology on decision making were briefly summarized. They are usually "givens" in an organization — not subject to short term adjustment. Still, they must be considered by the decision makers. The use of critical thinking is essential in order to make good decisions. Finally, the discussion of "theory versus reality" reinforces that all the different skills covered in this book should be useful to the decision maker, but no one should expect decisions to be as organized as the text suggests. Decision making can be a real dirty job, but we all have to do it.

Study Questions:

1. List several kinds of decisions a manager can allow a group to make, and others which the manager should make individually. What causes the difference?
2. What are some of the influences of organization structure on decision making?
3. What are some of the influences of technology on decision making?
4. How does framing influence a decision?
5. What are some things one must do to become a better critical thinker?
6. What is the value of theory in the decision making process?

Exercise:

Analyze a recent decision with which you are familiar.
- What was the process used in making it?
- Was adequate critical thinking used?
- Did any organizational structure, climate or cultural factors have an influence on the decision?
- Was technology an influence on this decision in any way?
- How else could the decision have been framed? Would that have influenced the result?

7

Developing Effective Change Proposals

"Whenever you set out to do something, something else must be done first."

– Murphy's Law, Corollary 6

Chapter Objectives:
This chapter is designed to enable the reader to ....
- Understand the steps in creating an effective change proposal.
- Effectively target a proposal to the proper audience.
- List and explain at least a dozen points which should be considered for inclusion in a change proposal.

I mplementing decisions and solving problems often means that you have to present your case to someone with the authority to make it happen. Successfully designing and presenting proposals for changes requires careful thought. The process recommended here can apply to proposals which are created by external consultants or internal staff employees or by individuals, supervisors or managers within the organization. The presentation to the decision maker may be in written or oral form, and the decision maker may be an individual manager or a group, such as an executive committee. The suggested proposal format which follows can also be applied to nearly any type of subject matter. An example proposal, including nearly all of the elements which are suggested in the discussion, is included at the end of the chapter.

Many projects will require more than one proposal and approval. So far in this book, we've come through the processes related to decision making and problem solving. The result of those actions will lead you to the next step of determining what sort of change appears to be necessary. A lot of information which would support a good change proposal may still be unknown until further along in the planning stages. If this is the case, you may need to first get approval to *design* the change or do further study, after which you'll have more information to go back for approval to *implement* the change.

Reasons a Proposal is Necessary

Managers require information to make decisions. This information may come from a variety of external or internal sources including staff, lower level managers, participative employee teams, or individual employees. Getting change recommendations implemented by management depends on making credible, effective proposals. Invariably, these proposals will include similar information, whether they are in written or oral form.

Regardless of how the information is conveyed, movement to and acceptance of any proposed change comes only when the decision maker is convinced of a valid need.

The focus of the presentation must be: *Why* is the change needed? If the "why" can't be sold, the "how" is irrelevant.

Ways to Improve the Acceptability of a Proposal

Solutions to problems and implementation of decisions will result in changes in the organization. Organizations tend to resist changes for the same reasons as individuals resist most changes. These include such concerns as cost of the changes, the fact that existing comfort levels and patterns are disrupted by change, and so on. Further, organizations often resist changes more than individuals. One reason is the physics concept of inertia: A body at rest tends to stay at rest; a body in motion tends to stay in motion in the same direction at a constant speed. Changing either of those takes energy, and the larger the body, the more energy it takes. Also, besides organizational inertia, there is something which might be called organizational immunization. In the biology of an organism, if something causes an unwanted change, the body will send defenses against it – white blood cells or whatever – to keep the change from happening. Organizations tend to do this, as well.

While most proposals will usually encounter some resistance, that resistance can be reduced by thoughtful and appropriate proposal design. In general, changes will be more easily accepted if they are:

- *as small as possible rather than radical.* This suggests that a one-day training program which will solve 70% of the problem will be more easily adopted than a week long program that may solve 90%.
- *reversible rather than permanent at first.* Suggest a pilot program, rather than a permanent, long term process.
- *the product of input from persons who have an interest in the subject.* See the following section for ideas.
- *timely.* Right after an announced budget cut is a good time to suggest cost saving ideas, but not ones which will add costs.
- *open to discussion rather than coming down as ultimatums.*

Decision makers of all kinds usually respond better to ideas which aren't totally new to them. Before any formal presentation or submission is made, the individual who is recommending the change should do some pre-selling. This may come about naturally as the proposal is designed. Make a conscious effort to involve:

- persons who will be affected by the change
- the decision makers, and
- the evaluators, who may be different persons than the decision makers.

Also, it may be wise to discuss the proposal with those who oppose it as well as those who favor it. The key to dealing with those who oppose it is to explain the proposal in generalities, but not in specifics. This can provide needed feedback, yet the lack of details will make it difficult for opponents to obstruct the idea.

The Level of Detail Needed Will Vary

In-depth development of the proposal and implementation plan has some benefits. Yet, deciding which people are to be moved first or exactly which shade of green to use for the handout folders has some hazards. It takes much longer to develop a complete proposal. It also commits the creator of the proposal to extensive efforts which may be wasted if the decision is "No" or "Yes, but..." instead of just "Yes." Besides, extensive details may murky the waters if the decision maker is interested only in the results, not the process.

Conversely, under-developed ideas may be harder to sell and may reduce the presenter's credibility in the eyes of the decision maker. They do, however, allow for easier adjustments and inclusion of improvements, as long as the decision maker is tolerant of less than completely developed plans. Get a decision on whether to develop the idea at all before getting into a discussion of how it will be implemented.

Be conservative in any estimates of the benefits. For example, let's say you want to propose a training program which is estimated to save $10,000 a year. You might, instead, propose it as saving, "...at least $7500." The lower figure may be more believable, thus less distracting to the flow of the presentation, and if it really saves $9,000, you are a hero instead of a bum for having overestimated the benefit.

Four Key Considerations in a Proposal

Design the Proposal Appropriately.

The level of formality of proposals will vary. As mentioned earlier in the book, the need for changes might be identified in many ways. The proposal, as well, may take the forms of a feasibility report, a suggestion system form, or an informal chat with the boss. The source of the issues which need change and the decision makers' general familiarity with those issues will influence how you approach and develop the proposal. Some of the first steps would be to:

Classify Your Audience.

Begin the design of a proposal by considering the audience which will be evaluating the recommendations. A useful way to think about this is to consider whether this person or group could be classified as an "Expert," "Technician," "Executive," "Layman" or "Combined" audience. The expert loves facts, will challenge any assumptions, and needs to be convinced on a theoretical level. The technician wants to know the mechanics and process of the proposal. The executive will look at the proposal from a management or cost/benefit or "value" perspective. The layman will be interested in the big picture, but will rely on the proposal for details and information at a more basic rather than technical level. The combined or unknown audience can best be addressed by compartmentalizing the proposal. This way, information of interest to each reader can be picked out without requiring complete review and understanding of the whole package.

Establish Your Credibility.

This step is sometimes unnecessary and sometimes impossible. You should, however, consider including some information to suggest that the proposed change is appropriate. If you or the individual or group which generated the idea for the change are well-known to the decision makers, you are probably stuck with your existing reputation – at least in the short run. If the reputation is good, be sure to keep it that way. If it's not, you may want to use additional sources to support your idea. At least you will know you need to carefully present and document your recommendations.

Credibility is, of course, in the eyes of the beholder. It always pays to scope out your audience and play to your strengths and their preferences as you design your proposal. Sometimes you can be more credible if you remind the decision maker of your MBA from Wharton; others may need to be reminded that you've done the job for five years and produced 120% of standard every quarter. Or, perhaps you can mention that your team's last three change suggestions were accepted and implemented at a savings of so many dollars. Sometimes showing that the idea has worked elsewhere in similar circumstances (maybe for a competitor?) will establish that it might be worth trying.

Whatever process you use, the key point is to maneuver the decision makers into a willingness to read about or listen to the idea. They have to believe that you may have something worthwhile to say.

Ensure a Focus on the Idea.

It has to be possible for the decision makers to get *to* the idea. One seldom finds jewelry in a rusted coffee can, though it can happen. One seldom expects, then, to find great ideas within sloppy presentations with catsup stains, misspelled words, or missing pages. On the other hand, an exquisitely produced, superbly printed and graphically memorable proposal which is shallow or unworkable will still not sell. Besides, if it's too slick, management will wonder why you spent so much time and money on the presentation instead of doing your job.

The objective of proposal packaging can be summed up by saying that it must be an "appropriate quality" for the situation at hand. Avoid distractions which will inhibit your message. This applies to both written and oral presentations.

Fourteen Categories Which Should Be Included (Or at Least Considered) in a Proposal

Not all of the categories suggested below are needed in each proposal. Depending on the topic and other circumstances, several of these ideas may be handled in a single sentence, while others may require pages or hours of discussion. The example proposal at the end of this chapter includes nearly all of these points, and is still less than a page long. These topics are presented in a sequence that will work for most proposals, but this is not sacrosanct. Rearrange them if it seems to make sense for the topic at hand.

Begin by Expressing the Need for a Change. State early and clearly *what* the proposal is and *why* it is needed. The only exception to this rule is if the proposal is so radical that stating it up front will result in an immediate rejection of the idea. In that situation, you will need to build up to the recommendation through discussion. Normally, though, that takes too much of the audience's time, so get right to the point. If this takes you more than three sentences, you need to rethink it and focus in more carefully.

Define the Problem or Opportunity Which Led to the Proposal. What brought this idea to mind? Remember, management frequently looks at problems or opportunities in terms of numbers. How much did it cost? How much more could be produced? How much time could be saved? The *"M" resources* might cue you to a way of defining the problem. What money, materials, methods, minutes (i.e., time), machinery, maintenance, management, markets, manpower, milieux, or manuscripts are doing less than they could? (OK – that's a stretch. Look up *milieux*, though, and you'll see why it works.)

Explain the Background on the Problem or Opportunity. How did the underlying problem or opportunity develop? Has it always been there, or did some change occur which has caused it?

Emphasize the Need for a Solution. What will happen if no changes are made? Will the organization still be able to operate? This "down-side discussion" needs to be tied to specific dollar and time costs whenever possible.

Specify the Benefits of Adopting the Proposal. What specific savings or improvement will occur as a result of implementing the change? Increased production, faster turnaround, reduced complaints, etc.? Once again, tying these to defensible and clear numbers will be helpful for most decision makers. You need to be enthusiastic about the benefits, yet not come across as a stereotypical used car salesman.

Note that the proposal details have still not been divulged. Presenting the benefits at this point in the suggested sequence is part of developing a momentum. The intent is to get the decision maker into a receptive enough mood to listen to the details. Subsequent headings specify these details, but you first need to sell the benefits which will come out of the proposed changes or ideas. It's a common technique taught in nearly every sales class. Once the benefits have been made clear, you can then move on to spelling out how these benefits can be achieved.

Define the Nature and Scope of the Proposal. What change is being proposed, and where will it be implemented? Does it involve one person, or one department or a company wide effort? How pervasive will the effects of the change be? What other areas of the organization will be affected in addition to the areas in which the change occurs? Who else, if anyone, needs to be involved?

Present a Plan for Implementation. What methods will be used in implementation? What tasks have to be done by whom? What facilities and equipment will be needed? When do these things need to happen? *Clarity* is the keyword in the implementation plan. Use analogy, example, simple graphics, and terms and formats comfortable to the audience. These might include charts, photographs, and tables.

The implementation plan, however, should include only the key points. Details can be included in an appendix for a written proposal or in handouts or visuals to be used only if needed during an oral proposal. This arrangement allows the presenter to engage in an unobstructed overview, yet drop to a deeper level, if necessary. The appropriate level depends on knowing the audience and whether the decision maker will be involved with simple approval/disapproval, or in the actual process of implementation.

Provide Support for the Proposal. Do you personally have any experience relevant to the proposal? Can you cite examples of where it has been tried before? Who else in the organization (or outside) may have the background to help? Are there any articles, books, or other reference sources you could cite to support the ideas? Remember to include those who helped develop the original idea and others in the organization with whom the proposal has already been discussed.

Discuss the Likelihood of Success. No implementation of change is going to come off perfectly. Of course, your proposal should have more going for it than against it, but don't leave yourself open to criticism by ignoring potential problems. It is far better to bring them up yourself than to respond to them only when challenged by the decision makers. Disarm this situation by listing possible criticisms and problems, with either a valid response to each or a summation of the consequences if these problems do interfere.

Explain and Justify the Cost of the Proposal. It is typical sales technique to leave discussion of the cost until the sale is made. Sooner or later, however, the issue of cost will come up. Be ready to present it accurately and in projected cost/benefit (value or ROI) terms. Remember, too, that total cost includes man-hours, materials, and many other things. In some organizations, the kind of cost may be as important as the amount of the cost. For example, a government agency may have budget for equipment but not for hiring people. It may be necessary to specify costs by category for this type of situation. Overall, do as much as possible to focus on the value created by the change.

Ask for a Decision. Incredible as it may seem, salespeople sometimes lose the sale simply because they don't ask the customer to buy. You need to ask for a decision. It will help to recap the main points, ask for questions, or offer clarifications and follow-up data. Set a deadline of when you'd like (or must have) the decision. You may also need to say whether or not the proposal can be modified or accepted in part. That is frequently, but not always, obvious.

Beware of too much pride of authorship. Decision makers often have information or agendas unknown to the persons who are proposing the change, so the questions and suggestions that come out of the presentation should be given serious consideration. Be willing to accept improvements, modifications and criticisms.

Include an Appendix. The term "appendix", of course, refers to an organ in the body that no one pays any attention to unless something goes wrong. It is frequently applied to written presentations and understood in those terms. It should include any supporting material which might be of interest to the decision maker, but which is so detailed that it would impede the flow of ideas. Examples of this could include charts, surveys, computations, input data, flow charts, articles, lists of personnel, etc. Similar information needs to be on hand or available for review following an oral presentation. The decision maker should be given some documentation for later review or as a reminder, in order to allow effective consideration of the proposal.

Be Prepared to Deal with the Decision. The proposal will probably generate a "Yes," "No," or a "Yes, but..." decision. Be sure you are ready to deal with any of the possible outcomes. Ask yourself what your next steps should be, and whether you should try again if you get a "No." Ask for and accept constructive feedback. Always continue to build your credibility. If the answer was "Yes," be sure to follow through and provide information on the results of the implementation. Remember, even the best ideas are useless without understanding and support from the decision makers.

Again, not all of the above categories will be needed for every proposal. Use it as a check list when you develop the proposal, and include the category only when it serves a purpose. See the following example of a simple proposal for a training program which incorporates most of these concepts.

An Example Training Proposal

MEMO

TO: J. P. Sousa, Executive Director
FROM: R. Vaughn, Training Department
DATE: January 19th
TOPIC: Proposal for Training

Sousa Industries needs to arrange a training program to improve the skills of our forklift operators. This need has resulted from two sources: (1) an increasing accident rate, and (2) new standards imposed by government regulation in this area.

First, our safety records show that lost time injuries for our forklift operators have gone up in each of the past three years at a rate faster than the increase in hours worked by persons in that job classification. While there may be various reasons for this, the supervisors report that at least part of the change is due to employee turnover during that period. Further, because this is apparently a state-wide trend, forklift drivers who handle hazardous materials (ours occasionally do) must soon be certified by the state commerce department.

A training program will help reduce the accident rate and associated costs, including employee medical expenses, damaged equipment, merchandise, and insurance costs. It will also prepare our employees for the upcoming certification process so that we can comply quickly with no loss in productivity.

This program should be provided for all current personnel in this job classification, and for others in related classifications who may occasionally fill in for our primary workers. All plant locations except Gainsborough are affected.

We propose using ACME Forklift Services as an external provider for this training. They have been in the business for six years, and are certified by the appropriate agencies to be in compliance with all standards related to the upcoming certification. They already have materials and training plans developed, and have provided excellent references from several companies in our industry.

The cost for this training will be approximately $380 per employee, plus mileage and any overtime incurred by their absence from the job. Training will be done off site at ACME's classroom in the Market Square area. This price includes all materials. If any of our employees who pass the ACME training do not pass the state certification, a free retraining session will be offered.

The total cost of approximately $6,400 will be charged against the operations budgets for each location.

We need your approval by the end of the month in order to set schedules for March. If you have any questions, contact me at my office (555-5432).

Summary

Many decisions, once made, require approval to implement. This means that the persons in authority must learn about and understand the need for action on the decision. A written or oral proposal is the common way for this information exchange to occur. Sometimes a proposal is even needed to get permission to do further study of the problem before a recommendation can be developed.

Proposals are, in essence, sales pitches, and there are ways to design them which will increase the likelihood of their being more readily accepted. These include making them as small as practical, well supported by those who will be affected, and so on. The person developing the proposal should work to establish their own credibility and design and present the ideas in ways that speak well to their audience.

Fourteen categories were suggested for inclusion in a proposal, along with some suggestions about how to develop each. While the actual nature of the proposal will be influenced by such things as the relationship between the proposer and the audience or the formality required due to the cost or organizational sensitivity to different ideas, this chapter provided a checklist which should be useful whenever a proposal is needed.

Study Questions

1. If an idea seems like it's too radical, how might you redesign it so it has a better chance of acceptance?
2. Name a couple of hazards of overdeveloping a proposal before it is presented.
3. If the person who will receive and decide on the proposal is an expert in the field, what sort of approach might you want to use? How about if he or she is a layman?
4. Why is it frequently appropriate to delay discussion of details about a proposal until later in the presentation?

Exercises

- Develop a practice proposal aimed at your boss to encourage him or her to do one of the following: (a) give you a raise; (b) move you to a larger office; or (c) buy your supplies or equipment from a different vendor.

The computer support provided with the book includes a downloadable/printable form for developing a proposal.

Note: The material in this chapter has been adapted from chapter 4 of *The Professional Trainer, 2nd edition* by Robert H. Vaughn ©2005, published by Berrett-Koehler Publishers, Inc., San Francisco.

PART II

The Toolbox

Each tool in Chapters 8 through 11 is presented in a similar format:

Name of the Tool

Overview: This defines where and when the tool should be used. What is its purpose, what special requirements are needed to use it, what does it do, and what doesn't it do? Helpful hints, areas to watch out for, and any additional information which applies are also included in this part. Other tools which are similar may be described here, or references are made to tools or appendices elsewhere in this book which may support this tool.

Knowledge or Input Required: What type of data must be collected, what sources might be appropriate, and any special techniques needed are listed here. Is it for group or individual use?

Results or Data Output: This explains what you get from using the tool.

Step by Step Instructions: What to do and how to do it.

Example(s): Which illustrate the steps described. At least one, and sometimes more examples are included for each tool.

In the *appendix* to the book, you will find information about *Mathematical Support and Software* for the tools. The mathematical formulae, along with how to apply it and any common software which can make it easier for you are described here. The disk included with the book also has forms preloaded for typical programs such as Microsoft Excel® and Microsoft Word®.

CHAPTER 8

Tools for Planning and Control

"Start with the end in mind."

– Steven Covey

Chapter Objectives:

This chapter is designed to enable the reader to ....
- Understand when and how to use Budgets.
- Understand when and how to use Control Charts.
- Understand when and how to use Gantt Charts.
- Understand when and how to use PERT Charts.

The tools in Chapter 8 relate to the concepts covered in Chapter 2.

Many of the tools described in this book can be used for parts of planning and control, but the ones covered in this chapter are primarily designed to help directly plan and control large projects or ongoing operations. This chapter covers four specific tools:

BUDGETING is a tool which is understood and used by nearly everyone. Only the basic principles are covered in this description. For further information, a book on personal finance is probably the best place to start. Though that will describe budgeting from a money point of view, the same principles apply to any sort of a budget.

CONTROL CHARTS are a specific form of scatter diagram in which time is one basis and the element to be controlled (quality, production, etc.) is the other. Like other scatter diagrams (described elsewhere in the book), they indicate the relationship between sets of data. They can also be effectively employed as concurrent or even forward looking control techniques.

GANTT CHARTS are named for their originator, Henry Lawrence Gantt (1861-1919). This is a forerunner of the PERT Chart, and is useful as both a planning tool and a control tool. It helps the manager organize data visually in a manner to improve decision making.

PROJECT EVALUATION & REVIEW TECHNIQUE (PERT) CHARTS were created by the Navy to help management of the complex development of the Polaris Submarine project. PERT is an expansion and interconnection of Gantt Charting, and like the Gantt Chart, can be used for both planning and control decisions.

A number of other tools which can also be used for planning or control are covered in subsequent chapters.

Tool #1: Budgets

Overview:

Budgets help a manager or team determine sources and uses of various types of resources necessary to accomplish a task. While typically associated with financial resources, the concept of a "budget" is also often applied to raw materials, time, and any other "expendable" resources which flow in and out of an organization. Management decisions of various kinds can be made using the budget as a tool.

For example, if a surplus is predicted, what ramifications does this create for the manager? If we're budgeting materials or supplies, a surplus may be undesirable, since it will cost money (space, insurance, etc.) to store in inventory. For a profit-making organization, of course, a surplus of dollars is probably an organizational goal. A surplus of time available means that too many people are working, or that more work needs to be found to keep them busy. Time, unlike money, can't be saved for future use, so the time budget should be designed to have equal sources and uses.

Conversely, if a deficit is predicted, management actions should be taken to develop other sources of income so the organization, project, or whatever is being budgeted, can continue to operate. Also, note that even if the sources and uses totals are equal, a problem may exist if the sources aren't available until after the uses are planned. So if you plan to spend $50,000 in a year, but it doesn't arrive until November 13th, you need to plan for 45 weeks of doing nothing and seven very busy weeks around Thanksgiving and Christmas. More realistically, a manager would need to find credit sources to deal with such a cash flow deficit.

Knowledge or Input Required:

To develop a budget, the manager or team must know where and when and how much of the resource will be made available for use, and what uses will be made of the resources over the time period covered by the budget.

Results or Data Output Provided:

A budget usually takes the form of a document which lists "income" and "expense" (i.e., the availability of and requirements for resources). Decisions can be made using the budget as input.

Step by Step Instructions:

Step 1: Define the resource to be budgeted. There must be a separate budget for each resource category. It's not logical, for example, to budget time, materials and cash on the same document.

Step 2: Define the period of time to be covered by the budget. Daily, weekly, monthly, quarterly, annual and total project time frames can be used.

Step 3: Determine the sources, categories, and arrival flow for the resource. Total the resource expected for the time period. Note any significant contingencies. For example, if some arrival times are uncertain or if arrival is dependent on some other event, this should be explained.

Step 4: Determine the uses, categories and distribution flow for the resource. Total the resource uses expected for the time period. Note any significant contingencies. For example, if some usage rates are uncertain, this should be explained.

Step 5: Compare the sources and uses totals. Note any differences. If sources exceed uses, a surplus of the resource will be available. If uses exceed sources, a deficit will exist.

Examples:

Both examples show budgets that have a surplus. Uses for the surplus should be determined. In example #1, the surplus is probably saved for a future project. The surplus in Example #2 may be left in the business in case projections aren't accurate, or in case future months' budgets show a deficit.

In general, most people are familiar with the concept of budgeting, so further treatment of it becomes superfluous. Note that, in an effort to avoid bad management examples, we chose not to use the Federal budget as an example. Suffice it to say that a surplus in the Federal budget has been almost as rare as a Cleveland Indians Pennant.

EXAMPLE #1: Materials Budget for Publishing a Company Report	
Sources	Uses
150 Sheets of Cover-weight paper	75 Front & 75 Back Covers
7500 Sheets of Standard 20# 8.5x11" paper	75 Page sets of 96 sheets each
2 packages (50 ea.) Plastic Comb Binders	1 per book for 75 books
Surplus: 300 sheets of paper and 25 binder combs.	

EXAMPLE #2: Cash Budget for May for Frank's Computer Service Business

Sources		Uses	
38 Repair jobs @ $1200 (avg.)	$ 45,600.	Labor: 3 Techs @ $22/hr	$ 10,428.
Minor Parts Sales	$ 3,350.	Supplies & materials	$ 12,520.
Less adjustments	$ -6,650.	Shop overhead (rent, etc.)	$ 8,210.
Net Sources:	$ 42,300.	Auto/Truck costs	$ 2,665.
		Owner's R.O.I.	$ 5,500.
		Other Expenses	$ 2,200.
		Net Uses:	$ 41,523.

Net Income: $777 (Surplus)

Tool #2: Control Charts

Overview:

Control charts are a special category of scatter diagrams (see Tool #16) which indicate relationships in successive data points over time. The horizontal (x-axis) component of a control chart is always time.

Knowledge or Input Required:

A basic understanding of the use of graphing is needed, along with information about the scales and data to be included along each axis.

Results or Data Output Provided:

Control charts help determine (1) whether or not a process is meeting standards, and (2) when plotted over time, what trends exist. This latter piece of information can allow the manager to predict problems (out of control situations) before they occur and to analyze past problems for possible causes.

Step by Step Instructions:

Step 1: Determine what operations need to be controlled. Collect sets of data to be compared. Make certain they're appropriately stratified to provide an accurate analysis.

("Stratified" means that the data is divided into appropriate categories.) You may want to stratify control charts by operator, by piece of equipment, by salesclerk, by shift, or whatever separation will later allow you to determine possible causes and remedies. The point of dividing the data is to make certain that the data provides enough analysis to determine trends and possible causes.

Step 2: On graph paper (or by some other appropriate means such as a computer program), lay out vertical and horizontal axes. Time is always shown horizontally, with earliest times at the left. While the technique can work with unconventional scaling, it interferes with effectively communicating the information to others.

Step 3: Place a dot or other mark at the intersection of the coordinates which represent each datum. (The word data is plural. A datum is a single piece of data.) See the examples on the following pages.

Step 4: Connect the points by drawing a line from first to second to third, etc. It may also be helpful to draw a light dotted line horizontally (parallel to the time axis) in order to see which dots are beyond the control limits. Look for trends in data, as well as points which are outside the control limits. See the examples which follow.

Control Charts show data and trends over time. They can be used with any information which represents measurements to be compared to standard. Examples could be:

- Percent returns for repair
- Number of out of stock parts requested
- Productivity of the workforce
- Percent of sales completed during calls
- Size of ball bearings produced
- Attendance of employees
- Customer complaint calls
- Et cetera

Examples:

Four simple examples are provided. Only the first is expanded with detail.

Example #1: Percent of Service Satisfaction

This sample control chart shows a record of cars which were brought in for service to a dealership which were done right the first time. The dealer had set a standard of no more than 10% returns on service appointments (therefore, 90% done satisfactorily) which is represented by the dashed line at 90%. Points below that are "out of control" and need to be investigated with corrective action taken. Points above the line are acceptable. The horizontal axis indicates time (hours, days, etc.) over which the data was collected. Thus, if you connect the dots, you have a visual pattern of how successfully the standard has been met.

In the example which follows, measurements were taken on selected days over a twelve week period to find the number of returns for service work which was not performed correctly. The standard was 90%. Only two times out of fifteen were below standard.

Management needs to know why the standard was not met on those days, and what corrective action needs to be taken. In order to know that, it might be necessary to trace the work back to a certain service technician or a certain kind of service requested. For this reason, the data collection needs to be set up in such a way as to allow later identification of any further information which might be needed.

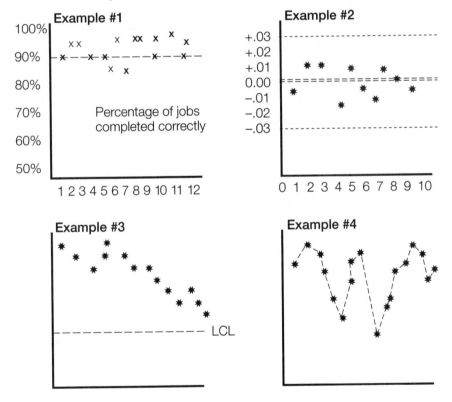

Control charts can provide visual indications of trends. Example #2 shows a relatively consistent pattern. Some ups and downs, but not extreme. All points are within the control limits of plus or minus 0.03. Unless high or low points are beyond the standards set, there's probably nothing to worry about. This chart shows both upper and lower control limits.

Example #3 shows an obvious downward trend over time. The process is still in control – no sample has yet reached the lower control limit. If we can predict that this trend will continue, we will want to make some adjustment *before* it gets out of control. Perhaps we're showing error rates. If so, the chart represents good news, but there would probably be no lower control limit on that type of a measurement – only an upper.

Example #4 shows wide swings from high to low. We should ask why these occur. If it represents customers to be serviced, for example, the highs and lows would have serious implications in our staffing needs. If we can't level out the pattern, we might want to consider using temporary help or in some other way trying to match our staff to the workload. If it represents quality levels, we really need to go into a problem solving mode and correct the wide variations. If it represents a stellar constellation, the artist is not very creative, and should read Chapter Four.

Tool #3: Gantt Charts

Overview:
This is a planning and control tool used to help schedule workload on various projects and see if they are being accomplished according to the schedule. It is named for its originator, Henry Lawrence Gantt, a production management pioneer.

Knowledge or Input Required:
Four things must be known in order to develop a Gantt Chart: (1) What activities must be accomplished during the scheduling time period. (2) Either when each of these must be started and/or when they must be finished. (3) How long each should take. (4) Whether or not starting of any activity is dependent on completion of another.

Results or Data Output Provided:
Using a Gantt Chart during the planning stages forces you to think through what events must happen over the scheduling period. The resulting chart is a quick visual reference allowing a check on the status of all projects in the schedule.

Step by Step Instructions:
Using the Gantt Chart as a Planning Tool

Step 1: Determine the limits of information you will include on the chart. What time period will the chart cover? That, of course, depends on the project you're charting. Less than a week is seldom helpful; more than a year becomes speculative. What range of activities will be included? Perhaps you'll include all major projects undertaken by the organization; maybe just those in a particular department; maybe just the activities which relate to one project. We'll use the example of building a house.

- Time period: The house should be built in sixteen weeks.
- Major activities: See list below.

Step 2: Prepare a chart with the activities listed down the left column, and a time line indicated along the bottom, as shown in the example.

Step 3: Draw a horizontal line or bar for each activity, starting at the point (above the time line) when the activity begins and finishing when it should end, according to schedule.

Step 4: Review to insure that any activity dependent on completion of another one does not start until the appropriate point. (E.g., the land must be completely acquired before the foundation can be dug.)

Construction Plan for 1234 South Street

Activity																
Acquire Land	■															
Dig Foundation		■	■													
Pour Concrete			■	■												
Put up framing				■	■	■										
Install Plumbing						■	■	■								
Install Electrical					■	■	■									
Basic Carpentry								■	■	■	■					
Drywall/Masonry								■	■	■						
Finishing Work											■	■	■	■		
Install Carpet														■	■	
SCHEDULED DATE (Weeks)	1	2	3	4	5	6	7	8	9	10	11	12	13	14	15	16

That ends the "planning" steps. As a control tool, you will periodically review the status, and indicate what portions of the projects are complete, versus the original plan. See the second Gantt Chart example.

Step by Step Instructions:
Using the Gantt Chart as a Control Tool

Step 5: As each activity is being accomplished, fill in, or in some way indicate progress on the bar for that activity on the chart. For example, the activity represented by the bar, below, is 50% finished.

Step 6: Draw a vertical line from the base, indicating today's date on the timeline.

Step 7: Visually compare to see which activities are ahead of or behind schedule. Take corrective actions, as appropriate.

In the example below, it is now day 2 of week 6 (indicated by the vertical line). The first three activities are completed. Some of the plumbing, electrical, and carpentry are done, but the framing is behind schedule. The carpentry work is ahead of schedule.

Corrective action, in this case, might include moving someone who's started doing the carpentry work to help with finishing off the framing work that's behind.

Construction Plan for 1234 South Street

Activity	1	2	3	4	5	6	7	8	9	10	11	12	13	14	15	16
Acquire Land	█															
Dig Foundation		█	█													
Pour Concrete			█	█												
Put up framing				█	█											
Install Plumbing					█	█	█									
Install Electrical					█	█	█	█								
Basic Carpentry							█	█	█	█	█					
Drywall/Masonry							█	█	█	█						
Finishing Work											█	█	█	█		
Install Carpet														█	█	█
SCHEDULED DATE (Weeks)	1	2	3	4	5	6	7	8	9	10	11	12	13	14	15	16

Tool #4: Program (or Project) Evaluation & Review Technique "PERT Charts"

Overview:

PERT Charts are a planning and control tool which can help structure information for decision making. They are an extension of Gantt Charts and useful for much more complex projects. When combined with the Critical Path Method, they dramatically reduce the need for comprehensive control of a project. If the project has various activities which are interdependent, meaning that one must be completed before another is started, PERT Charts can be effective. If there is no or very little interdependence, Gantt Charts will be more appropriate.

It takes time to make up a PERT Chart, so they're not recommended for simple projects. As you would expect, computer software is available to assist this process. It usually comes under the heading of "Project Management " software.

Each activity in a PERT Chart must flow from the "start" box and to the "finish" box. No activity can dangle; there must be a line into and out of each activity box except for the start and finish boxes.

If a line comes from one box into another, that means that the activity in the first box must be completed before the activity in the second box can begin. All activities in boxes on lines into any given activity box must be completed prior to the start of the activity in that box. If there is no such relationship, the boxes should be on separate paths, not sequential on the same path.

PERT Charts depict the way in which activities *must* happen. They are not a chronology of simply the way we *choose* to do things. For example, in a PERT Chart depicting cleaning up the house, we could do laundry before or after dusting. Since there's no relationship between these, they should be on separate paths. On the other hand, we must pick up the kids' toys before we can vacuum the rug, so those things should be on the same path with the pick up toys activity shown first.

Complicated PERT Charts might have hundreds of activity boxes included.

Knowledge or Input Required:

To create a PERT Chart, you must know: (1) What activities are necessary to complete the project, and in what order, and (2) How long each activity should take. Probably one of the most practical approaches is to begin with a Gantt chart, then develop the PERT chart from there.

Results or Data Output Provided:

The PERT Chart, once completed, serves as a visual project guide and reference tool. It indicates the required paths of progress toward completion of the project. Determining the critical path allows management by exception for many to most activities in the project. An activity which is not on the critical path will have some slack time, so that even if it is delayed, the entire project will not be delayed. Therefore, managing these activities is not as critical. They need to be reviewed less frequently and need corrective action only when they are seriously behind schedule. Management control efforts should be focused on those activities which are on the critical path.

Several pieces of information are *not* readily apparent from a PERT Chart as shown in this text. The simple PERT Chart does not readily depict costs. It also doesn't show which work is done in-house and which is subcontracted, nor whether the work is subject to any internal delays. The length of the line between events is not necessarily proportional to the actual time (unlike a Gantt Chart). If the chart shows five days required to do an activity, you don't know (from just looking at the chart) if more people could do it in less time, or if the five days is based on true time requirements such as needing to let concrete dry or medicine take effect, etc. More complex PERT Chart formats can also help to control costs, human resource assignments, and so on, but the ones shown in this book are limited.

Step by Step Instructions:

Using a PERT Chart for Planning

Step 1: Define the project to be covered by the PERT Chart.

Step 2: List each of the events, start to finish, which must occur to complete the project.

Step 3: Begin by making a box marked "Start," on the left side of a sheet of paper. To the right of that, make a vertical column of boxes listing each of the events from step 2 which can be immediately started, i.e., that has no other step which must come first. Draw a line or lines from the "Start" box to each of these. (You may use code numbers for each event in the activity boxes, rather than rewriting titles of each event. This is less readable on major projects, but it works.)

Step 4: To the right of each of these boxes, make another set of boxes listing activities which require only one or more of those events in the second column to be completed before they can be started. Draw a line or lines from each of the boxes in column two to those in column three which require their completion. Continue in this fashion until all events are listed. Draw a final box marked "Finish." Identify all boxes which as yet have no exit lines, therefore need not be completed prior to anything else on the chart being started. Draw lines from these into the final box.

Step 5: Along each of the lines between boxes, estimate the time necessary to complete all activities related to the first event before the next can start. Write this time above or next to the line. Keep the units constant (hours, days or whatever). Remember that even though several events can be worked on simultaneously, you may have limited human resources which would prevent you from accomplishing all activities as fast as any one line would indicate.

This completes the basic planning function. You may then need to determine resources to apply to the project based on this plan. For example, who needs to be involved, what kind of equipment will they need, how much should each activity line cost, etc.?

Step by Step Instructions:

Using a PERT Chart for Control

To use the PERT Chart for Control, *Steps 1–5* from above must first be completed.

Step 6: As each event happens, indicate along the line that the activity has been completed. Check the time and cost as the activities progress. You need to have the objectives and standards predetermined. As you measure performance and evaluate, you will also have some possible causes of variation and corrective actions in mind, if variation does occur.

Step 7: Determine the critical path (Optional, but recommended for complex projects). To do this, follow all sequences of events from START to FINISH to find which path has the longest expected time for completion. This is the Critical Path. What this means is that any event in this sequence which is delayed causes a delay in the entire project. Any event not on the critical path has some slack. The net result of this is that if you carefully manage those events on the critical path, you can manage all others by exception. Check on them occasionally, and don't worry about them unless they get considerably behind schedule. On a large PERT chart, this may mean you only need to carefully manage 5-10% of the events.

Example:

Human Resources Planning Study Implementation Plan

This example is a human resource planning and career development project from a division of a large company. It was a seven month project. The events on the critical path are indicated by heavier outlines on the activity boxes.

The critical path estimated time is 148 working days (7 months). That means the project could be finished in 7 months if different people are working on the different paths. If one person has to do everything, the PERT Chart still shows the sequence, but the time from start to finish will be the total of all times on the chart, not just the critical path time. In this example, a total of 278 days of work are indicated, but they can be done in 148 days start to finish.

Notes to the example on page 103:

- The arrows show the direction of the path.
- A shaded box indicates activities on the critical path.
- Numbers along a path indicate the estimated number of working days needed to complete moving from one activity to the next.
- Some purists might object to the graphic being drawn so that some arrows go left. Ideally, all arrows should go right or down. Please note the length of the line does not indicate the length of time to complete the activity.
- It's also possible to put cost estimates along each of the lines as well as time. This can become more complicated, of course, but does provide additional control.
- We predict writing the draft of the company policy will take seven days. This activity is not on the critical path. If it happens to take a little more or less, no problem. We don't need it until the 15th day when we plan to make our presentation to the Executive Staff. It's only if it gets way behind (8 days or more) that it could affect the final completion date of the project. If an activity on the critical path gets behind schedule even one day, either the time must be made up or the entire project is delayed.

Other Planning and Control Tools

Only four tools have been included in this chapter. Many other tools described later in this book are also appropriate for planning and control, as are many not covered in this book. The reader is referred to appropriate textbooks on principles of management (listed in the bibliography) if there is further interest. The computer support disk also includes additional PERT examples which may be simpler to follow.

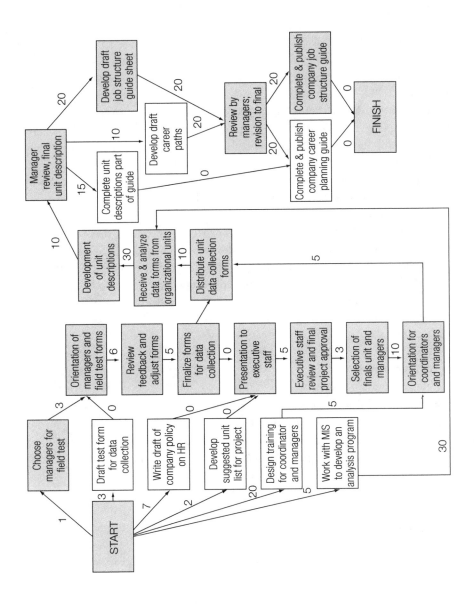

Summary

This chapter has presented the first four of nearly two dozen tools in this text. Gantt Charts, PERT Charts, and Budgets all can be used for both management planning and control. As they are being created, they force planning to happen in a systematic way. The manager or analyst must work through the process step by step in order to develop the chart or budget. As explained in Chapter Two, the manager must establish objectives, set limits, develop options, evaluate those options, choose the best, then implement the plan. This thoroughness will make all of the following stages of management easier. If the plan has not been thoroughly developed, then the organizing, directing and controlling will be more difficult.

Once these tools have been developed as part of the planning, they can then be used in the control process. All of them provide means to complete the four steps of the control process: Establish standards (done during the planning stages), Measure performance, Compare and evaluate, and Correct the problems, if any. Tool #2, Control Charts, isn't part of a planning mode, but does work well to help visualize the standards and keep track of the measurement results in the control process.

Study Questions:

1. Which two of the four tools covered in this chapter can be used for financial control?
2. Which of these tools uses an element of time?
3. When would you use a PERT Chart in preference to a Gantt Chart?
4. How do Control Charts provide for "forward looking" control processes?
5. What sorts of resources can be controlled using a budget?

Exercises:

- List some activities you might want to control using a control chart with (1) an upper control limit only; (2) a lower control limit only; (3) both an upper and lower control limit. How did you determine which applied?
- Make a Gantt Chart for planting a garden using at least eight activities.
- Translate that Gantt Chart into a PERT Chart.
- Make a personal financial budget for yourself or your household for next month. At the end of the month, check how accurate it was.

9

Tools for Creativity

"Too often, our minds are locked on one track. We are looking for red – so we overlook blue. Many Nobel Prizes have been washed down the drain because someone did not expect the unexpected."

– John D. Turner

Chapter Objectives:

This chapter is designed to enable the reader to ....

- Understand how and when to use brainstorming and its variations.
- Understand how and when to use cause-effect analyses.
- Understand how and when to use checklists.
- Understand how and when to use attribute listing.
- Understand how and when to use morphological analyses.
- Understand how and when to use catalog techniques.
- Understand how and when to use artificial intelligence.
- Be aware of a variety of other creativity tools which might be used.

The tools in Chapter 9 relate to concepts discussed in Chapter 4.

Each of the tools in this chapter is designed to help decision makers and problem solvers generate options from which they will later choose the best. Very seldom will any of these tools give you an absolute answer. They *will* provide information to *help structure* your decision making, but the final decision usually involves a certain amount of risk.

These tools come in a variety of forms. Some can be used by an individual. Some require group interaction. Some focus on certain types of problems or decisions, while others are generic and seem to be applicable to nearly any issue. You may have heard of and used some of these before. Some are so intuitive that you may have used them and never even thought about it being a tool for creativity.

When you are faced with a problem to solve or decision to make using one of these tools, you are encouraged to carefully follow the steps suggested in this chapter. As mentioned before, it may sound contradictory to suggest that being structured can make you more creative. It's really not, though, since we know that structure and discipline are necessary to excel at most human endeavors. Simply put, having a tool and knowing how to use it can make the task easier.

The tools included in this chapter are:

BRAINSTORMING. One of the mainstays of business people for many years was created by Alex Osborne. It uses a group process to generate a wide variety of ideas quickly. The purpose is quantity, not quality. It's easy to do, and often successful, even when done poorly. It does have a discipline to the process, as described here. There are also certain conditions under which it doesn't work well. Some variations on the general concept of brainstorming have been developed to reap the benefits of the process even in conditions where the classic style doesn't work. Two examples of these are the so-called Nominal Group Technique and the Gordon Technique, also called reverse brainstorming.

CAUSE–EFFECT ANALYSES. This tool also can assume a variety of forms and applications. It can be an input-output diagram, a "fishbone" diagram, or a simple table of causes and effects. Which of these is appropriate depends on the subject matter at hand. Courses in logic or critical thinking teach cause-effect tables as a process to insure that your thinking is accurate. So for problem solving, simply putting down on paper what you know to be causes and results of each other can show you where more information may be needed or where your thinking may be fuzzy. Trying to generate ideas, though, would lend itself more to fishbone diagrams. Presenting ideas to upper management may be best through an input-output diagram.

CHECKLISTS. These are another way of tapping into work that someone else has already done for us. These, like the catalog technique (below), come in a variety of shapes, sizes and purposes. Perhaps the best creativity checklist ever developed is among the examples which are included. A variety of sources for others is also suggested.

ATTRIBUTE LISTING. Since a big perception barrier is that we see what we expect to see, attribute listing is a tool to help us look at things in a different way. A common technique for this is to break some "thing" into component parts. This thing could be a problem or it could be something physical such as a product you're trying to improve.

MORPHOLOGICAL ANALYSIS. The name might cause you to expect this one to be contagious. It was created by Dr. Fritz Zwicky and Dr. Myron Allen and is, in a way, the opposite of Attribute Listing. Instead of breaking things into parts, you use this by forcing combinations. It's a useful technique. It's slightly hazardous, though, with the advent of computers since one can get carried away in making too many forced combinations. A couple of good examples and one extreme example are shown.

CATALOG TECHNIQUE. We do this unconsciously (and haphazardly) on an almost daily basis. Using catalogs allows us to take advantage of research that thousands of others have done for us. We can use the "classic" catalogs such as the J.C. Penney Catalogs, or encyclopedias or lots of other reference documents created just for the purpose of helping our creativity! Today's "catalogs" include the myriad of databases and on-line resources available through the internet / world-wide web or a company intranet. The discussion also suggests some ways of tapping into this often underutilized source of creative ideas.

ARTIFICIAL INTELLIGENCE. This is the one exception in the book to the "no computers needed" rule. It's included in the academic version of this text because it is good material for a project. Moreover, A.I. is coming into much wider use in general business applications, so managers should be familiar with the concept. Some software design packages for A.I. are quite user friendly. Most are user friendly, once they've been set up by an expert.

OTHER CREATIVITY TECHNIQUES. Guided fantasies (also under a variety of names with their own originators). Doodling. (Yes!) Relaxation Play. Non-Verbalizing. Free Associating. Lots & lots of options exist, and you can even add your own. A few others are discussed briefly at the end of the chapter.

Tool #5: Brainstorming & Variations

Overview:

Brainstorming and its common variations are used as creative, inductive or idea generating tools. Brainstorming can be applied to nearly any situation where alternatives must be developed, whether for planning or problem solving. *Group interaction is required.* (Other techniques are discussed later in the chapter which can be used by an individual.)

Ground rules for effective use of Brainstorming include the following:

- *Size of the group*. Groups smaller than 4 or larger than ten become awkward and less productive. Larger groups should be subdivided. Smaller groups might try some other techniques or temporarily add other people who might have some worthwhile perspective on the problem.
- *Mix of the group*. Homogeneous groups tend to produce uncreative ideas. When possible, use a group for brainstorming which is varied in background, age, job category, etc. The diversity will usually enhance the creativity generated.
- *Quantity of ideas is the goal*. This means that you go for volume, not quality of ideas. The participants should be encouraged to combine ideas, improve on each others' ideas, hitch hike on things already suggested, etc.
- *No evaluation of ideas or negative thinking*. That's reserved for the next step in the decision making stage, not now. Evaluation at this point tends to inhibit people from being free flowing.
- *Intentionally wild ideas*. Sometimes throwing out a few completely off the wall ideas will loosen up a group and encourage alternative viewpoints. Some leaders start with a silliness session to get the creativity juices flowing. (It doesn't work for everyone, though.)
- *Limit the time*. About 15 minutes at least, and 45 minutes at most.
- *Don't discuss the issue ahead of time*.

Jobs of the group leader for Brainstorming:

- Make sure all participants know and follow the ground rules.
- May use warm up techniques to get the group participating.
- May also need to define the problem and set the structure by which you'll proceed.
- Keep the discussion "on track".
- Record ideas in a way they can be viewed by the group (flip chart, computer display, etc.)
- If you paraphrase as you write the idea, confirm with the person that you've captured the essence of what they intended.
- Participate, if desired, but don't judge or edit the ideas.

Potential problems or cautions with Brainstorming:

- The group can inhibit the members. Skillful leadership or structure may be needed to insure everyone's participation toward the most effective list of alternatives.
- The members can inhibit the group. For example, an expert or a higher-level manager as a team member may discourage others from participating.
- Too much play or getting off track.
- Criticism or negative thinking, even subtle, can ruin the effectiveness of the process.
- Homogeneity of the group which all thinks alike or has worked together can inhibit creativity.
- Effective leadership and group facilitation is essential.
- Doesn't work well for decisions with high risk or uncertainty.

Common Variations in Brainstorming:

Structured Brainstorming can combat problems such as one person dominating the discussion or others not contributing. Once the problem has been described, each person is asked to contribute one idea at a time in turn. If he or she doesn't have an idea, they pass. This continues until everyone has passed in the same round.

Nominal Group Technique can be used to allow individual creativity to work before it becomes inhibited by the group. This process requires people to think silently, first, writing down their ideas. They then contribute to the list in round-robin style. Each person can question the contribution to clarify what is meant, but should not challenge or analyze it. NGT also ends with a voting process which asks people to choose their favorite several (one to five) ideas, thereby giving the group a sense of popularity of the ideas, once they've been presented. This voting either narrows down the number of options to consider in the next decision making step, or actually begins the analysis. It can be used with traditional brainstorming, as well.

Gordon Technique can be used when the problem might suggest "obvious" solutions to the participants, thereby inhibiting creativity. For example, if we have a problem that's always been dealt with in one way, it's natural to block out other ways of doing it. In this process, the group is called together to come up with ideas about a subject *known only to the leader*. The leader starts with a very broad and abstract definition of the problem, getting responses to that, then subsequently narrowing the statement through several stages, each time retaining previous suggestions which still apply to the narrower statement. (An example is given later in this section.)

Brainwriting is a variation where each person gets a sheet of paper and anonymously writes their ideas on the question under discussion. After a few minutes, each person passes their sheet on to the next person who elaborates and adds any more of their own ideas suggested by what they just received. The sheet then goes on to the next person until all people have contributed to each original list.

What to do with the lists:

The purpose of Brainstorming is to create extensive lists, and because evaluation during the process is prohibited, the result is — of course — lots of ideas, many of which are likely to be impractical or impossible to use.

To make the lists usable, the ideas must be objectively evaluated. First, eliminate any truly unworkable ideas. CAUTION: The person making this decision will approach it with his or her biases. Be sure the idea is actually unworkable before it's eliminated. The remaining ideas should be grouped and similar ones combined. The grouping is so we can determine what information needs to be collected to evaluate them, and where the same information can be used on more than one evaluation. Finally, a priority should be established as to which ones get evaluated first. The basis for the priority might be cost (which ones are cheapest, for example), likelihood of success, ease of evaluation, or whatever makes sense to the decision makers.

Group evaluation of the ideas:

Many of the ideas may be workable, and perhaps more than one will be used. If the analysis of which is best isn't too complicated, it may be practical to use the brainstorming group to narrow down the options or even choose which to use. A means of doing this (mentioned in the NGT paragraph above) is to take a vote.

Let's say that 45 ideas were generated by the brainstorming process. The leader could ask everyone to look over the list and choose the five they think will work best. After everyone's had a few minutes to do this, a vote is taken on each item with each person getting five votes. The result is a list of favorites, based on which ones got the most votes.

This process will only work when the group itself has adequate information to make the evaluation. It tends to be a popularity contest among the ideas, rather than a quantitative or objective evaluation. But, if any number of ideas will actually work to solve the problem, then the most popular one might be a reasonable choice.

Knowledge or Input Required:

The leader must know the general nature of the problem or plan for which alternatives are needed and the techniques described below.

Results or Data Output Provided:

Brainstorming creates extensive lists of alternatives, some or all of which will be applicable to the problem or plan at hand. It does not directly evaluate the quality of the alternatives; techniques in Chapter 10 may be used for that purpose.

Step by Step Instructions:

Step 1: Define the problem or situation requiring alternatives.

Step 2: Convene a group for brainstorming.

Step 3: Explain the problem or subject to the group.

Step 4: Use warm up techniques, if desired; structure the process, if appropriate.

Step 5: Have the group generate ideas on the subject.

Step 6: Leader lists the ideas on a flip chart or other visual so all participants can see them.

Step 7: Acceptable ideas are then subjected to appropriate decision making techniques.

Examples:

Example 1: Getting Workers for Saturday Overtime

A company which manufactured synthetic quartz crystals had always relied on employees who volunteered for paid overtime, rather than specifying who had to stay late or come in on Saturdays. This had worked well, but orders were up and volunteers weren't. Management chose not to require overtime, but wanted to encourage more people to volunteer. This issue was put to the supervisors in the form of a brainstorming issue.

The suggestions were slow at first, since the supervisors had kind of dealt with this problem for years and were locked into how it had always been done. The leader (from outside the group) finally threw in a few off the wall ideas including a free keg of beer at lunch (quitting time) on Saturday. The group laughed, and a couple tried to better that with their own wild ideas. Thus loosened up, the group went on to list the following:

Appeal to the "company spirit"
Free coffee on weekends
Allow flex-time on weekends
Provide a bonus for every four Saturdays worked
Explain the need for overtime
Allow choice of jobs within classifications on weekend
Competition between departments
Etc.

The favorites were voted on at the conclusion of the session, and several were going to be tried that week. The one that worked best was to explain to the workers that the workload had really increased and that people were actually *needed* on Saturdays, unlike in the past when the time was useful but not essential.

Example 2. Reverse Brainstorming (also called Gordon Technique) for an Ad Campaign

A small company which sold a service to a mostly local customer base had always used newspaper advertising. To expand their business, the marketing director wanted to try some other media. Everyone in the company, if asked directly, would say that the newspaper is the best way to advertise, so it seemed probable that brainstorming would not be a good approach to new idea generation.

At a weekly management meeting, a consultant took the management team through a reverse brainstorming. (The marketing director did not lead it, as the objective might have been too obvious, thus undercutting the technique.) The question was thrown out to the group: "When you need to get someone's attention, how do you do that?" This abstract and broad question resulted in responses of "Yell", "Tap them on the shoulder", "Whisper", "Flash a light", and many others. These were recorded on the flip chart. The group was then asked, "How do you get people to do things you want them to do?" Another list was made. "How do you learn about things?" Now three lists were on the charts, and the consultant narrowed the focus: "How do you learn about dry cleaning?" This was a parallel service to what the company provided, but to the same general kind of a market as their company served. It allowed the managers to see themselves as customers rather than suppliers, and the lists on the board provided fuel for ideas which they had used as customers.

Finally, the specific question emerged, "How else should our company promote its service?" The list which resulted was probably far more creative than would have come from a traditional brainstorming exercise.

112

Tool #6: Cause - Effect Analyses

Overview:

Cause - Effect Analyses can be done in a variety of ways. Their purpose is to find and/or confirm relationships between facts. The "cause" part can be used to help search for causes of problems (variances from standard) in control. The "effect" part can be used to help project what might happen as a result of implementing plans. These diagrams can also be used to help organize Brainstorming (Tool #5) as it is being done. Further, much of the value of these tools is to get down on paper the "facts" and relationships as we believe them to exist. Having them laid out visually helps to follow the logic and test it for reasonableness.

Common Technique Variations in Cause-Effect Analyses:

Basic "Fishbone" Diagrams One of the most common formats for cause-effect analyses looks something like a fish skeleton, hence the name "fishbone."

Input-Output Diagrams Input-Output diagrams are similar to cause-effect diagrams, except that both ends are shown, and the "black box" activity or event in the middle is analyzed.

Tables or Chains Cause - Effect Tables or Chains are listings which allow us to follow the logic of thought patterns relating to management decisions or problem solving. The reason for the name becomes apparent in the example below. Sometimes, simply listing on paper a cause and the possible effects or an effect and the possible causes will be helpful in structuring your thinking about a problem or list of possible alternatives.

Matrix (Johari Window) Cause-Effect Matrices give a quick visual summary of the results of data analyses, and can suggest relationships, or lack thereof, between potential cause and effect.

Each of these is described in the paragraphs below.

Knowledge or Input Required:

The decision maker or problem analyst must know the general nature of the problem or plan which needs to be analyzed and the steps described below. If a group is involved in using the tool, brainstorming techniques (Tool #5) could be useful in coming up with lists of possible causes or effects.

Results or Data Output Provided:

Cause - Effect diagrams use a graphical (visual) format of lines and tables designed to represent a meaningful relationship between an effect and its causes or a cause and its resulting effects. They can be used to: (1) Recognize important causes, (2) Understand all effects and causes, (3) Compare operational procedures. (4) Improve processes, and (5) Determine options or possible solutions. These tools are frequently taught as part of a total quality management or SPC orientation.

For Basic Cause-Effect "Fishbone" Diagrams
Step by Step Instructions:

Step 1: Draw a horizontal line with an arrow at the right hand end and a box in front of it. The effect or problem should be written in the box. For example:

Step 2: Write the major possible causes (example: material, method, worker, machine, etc.) in boxes placed parallel to and some distance from the main arrow. Connect the boxes by arrows slanting toward the main arrow. For example:

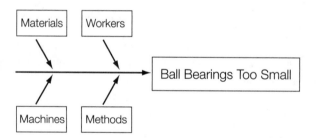

Step 3: List the minor causes on the chart around the major causes which they affect. They are connected to the major causes on lines or arrows pointing into the major causes. These can be generated by brainstorming techniques (Tool #5), checklists (Tool #7), or any other creativity technique which might result in an effective list of possible causes. For example:

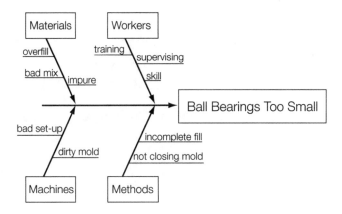

You can readily see why the name "fishbone diagram" has been applied to this technique. Using this process on a flip chart or white board allows a visual arrangement and structuring of ideas. Additional ones can be added as they are suggested.

The same technique can be used to look at various effects from a cause. Simply put the box at the left, and draw the arrows out the right side. You might try drawing one with the left box showing a cause of "Quit my job", and the effects including such major ones as financial, personal, family, etc.

For Input-Output Diagrams
Step by Step Instructions:

Step 1: As above, begin with a box, but this time with arrows into and out of it. The fishbone on the input side is made up of causes; the one on the right of effects. The box can represent some known or unknown activity, event or process. See the example below for an Input-Output Diagram of "Better Hotel Management Policy."

Step 2: Again, list possible major causes and major effects of a better hotel management policy in boxes.

Step 3: As before, list possible factors influencing or resulting from each box. Continue to subdivide and list further effects, if appropriate.

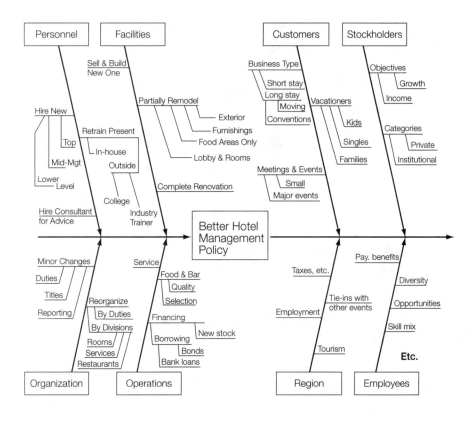

For Cause-Effect Table or Chain Diagrams

Step by Step Instructions:

Step 1: Make a simple table, such as shown below, with the headings "*Cause*" and "*Effect.*"

Step 2: Begin with whichever (the cause or the effect) you have the most information about, and put it in the correct side

Step 3: Work logically to try to determine the effect (or possible effect) from the cause or vice versa.

Cause	Effect
Cause A	Effect B
Cause C	Effect D
Cause E	Effect F
etc.	etc.

Or instead of a table, you might find it useful to just put on paper the sequence of causes which result in effects which result in further causes & effects. For example:

Cause A | Effect B | Cause C | Effect D / Cause D | Effect E … etc. OR

or

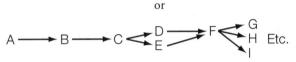

They aren't always linear, of course; a cause may have more than one arrow out of it. You may find several causes or possible causes to the same effect or result. You may also find several effects/results from individual causes. They'll also daisy chain around, with one effect becoming a cause of something else. This may bring to mind the famous camp song about getting some water from the well, when the bucket has a hole in it. If you missed that one as you grew up, find a cub scout and ask him.

For Cause-Effect Matrix Diagrams (Also called Johari Windows)
Step by Step Instructions:

Step 1: Draw a 2 by 2 box, as shown below, and list headings on each side. The vertical axis can be the possible causes, and the horizontal the possible effects. The simplest form uses "Yes" and "No" headings, as shown.

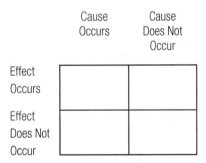

Step 2: Collect data on whether or not the cause and effect exist together in your research. Where the cause exists, does the effect? Where the effect exists, does the cause? For each case mark the appropriate box in the matrix as shown in the example.

Step 3: Analyze the results. If most of the marks in the boxes are in just two boxes which are diagonally opposite from each other (such as on the next page) you can imply that there may be a cause and effect. If your marks are spread among all four boxes, you can imply that there is no cause and effect.

Example:

We are investigating whether there is a cause effect relationship between being female and liking horses. We define "being female" as the possible cause, and "liking horses" as the effect. Then we talk with 40 people and ask if they're female (be prepared for nasty comments if you have to ask), and if they like horses. We then tally the results in each box according to the answers. If we have taken an honest sample (see Chapter Five), we can imply a rather strong cause - effect relationship from this data.

	Cause Occurs	Cause Does Not Occur
Effect Occurs	✓✓✓✓✓ ✓✓✓✓✓ ✓✓✓✓✓ ✓✓✓✓	✓✓✓
Effect Does Not Occur	✓✓	✓✓✓✓✓ ✓✓✓✓✓ ✓✓✓✓✓ ✓

Tool #7: Checklists

Overview:

Like several of the other tools in this chapter, checklists can be either inductive or deductive. Therefore, they can be used to either create options or evaluate them, depending on the nature of the checklist.

Some checklists require a step by step approach (such as putting together the swing set you bought your kid), while others essentially serve as pre-constructed brainstorming lists and require no specific sequence. Both types can be useful.

Typical checklists might deal with:

• Items you'll need for vacation
• How to set up your computer
• What automobile maintenance is needed at 36,000 miles
• What groceries you might need for the week

Essentially, any pre-constructed list of points to consider is a checklist. They can be beneficial since they are reusable and allow you to take advantage of other people's ideas on the subject (or your own previous ideas).

Knowledge or Input Required:

Where to find effective checklists. Common sources for effective checklists include the following:

- Textbooks on the subject
- Published articles on the subject
- Advertisements about a product or service
- Owners or Instruction Manuals
- Etc.

(This, by the way, is a checklist)

Results or Data Output Provided:

Using checklists helps the decision maker to add structure to either creative or analytical processes. Essentially, they provide a means to use others' thinking to help the process along. The checklists simply provide suggestions for consideration in specific applications.

Step by Step Instructions:

Step #1: Find a checklist that matches the need & Use it.

Examples:

The example checklists which follow deal with things germane to decision making and problem solving.

Perhaps the best "generic" or "all purpose" checklist ever developed comes from The Creative Engineering Laboratory at Massachusetts Institute of Technology. It includes many idea-spurring questions which can prompt us in almost any inductive situation. It's given in a condensed form below. Some of the examples will, of course, seem outdated, but you should be able to follow most of them from their original form.

One other checklist has been included which several students have told me they've used over and over in their jobs.

Example #1: The M.I.T. Creativity Checklist

OTHER USES?

- New Ways to Use As Is? (Like using helicopters to patrol high tension lines over mountains.)
- Other Ways, if Modified? (Like the wallboard manufacturer which added a line of jigsaw puzzles.)

- How About Salvaging? (Like the rubber company which found that wasted strips of surgical tubing could be sold as rubber bands.)
- What Other Use Could Be Added? (Like telephone companies installing recordings to furnish the latest time and temperature.)

BORROW OR ADAPT?

- What Else Is Like This? (Like the studies of birds made by aircraft pioneers.)
- What Parallels Does the Past Provide? (Like what modern dress designers do in devising new creations from ancient art.)
- Could Other Processes Be Copied? (Like the Japanese technique of copying nature by sticking grains of sand into oysters to produce genuine pearls.)
- What Other Ideas Might Be Adaptable? (Like Diesel, who got his engine ideas from a cigar lighter.)

GIVE IT A NEW TWIST?

- What Other Shape? (Like the buggy maker who tapered the roller bearing which had been invented 400 years earlier by Leonard da Vinci.)
- What Other Form? (Like detergent powders instead of bars of soap; or liquid soap instead of either.)
- How To Create New Looks? (Like shoes that show women's toes.)
- What Could Color Do? (Like what the automobile industry did in 1955 to make it the biggest new-car year in history.)
- How About Motion? (Like Christmas tree lights that bubble.)
- How About Sound? (Like a clothes dryer which shuts off singing, "How Dry I Am.")

MORE SO?

- Longer Time? (Like the baker who featured slow baked bread.)
- Greater Frequency? (Like the doctor who originated the idea of lighter but more frequent meals for ulcer victims.)
- Increase Strength? (Like reinforced heels and toes in hosiery.)
- Increase Height? (Like circus clowns on invisible stilts.)
- Greater Width? (Like the center strip on newer superhighways.)
- Include Plus Ingredients? (Like fluoride in drinking water or toothpaste.)

LESS SO?

- What If Lower? (Like the recent trend in motor cars.)
- What If Narrower? (Like men's ties, lapels, hat rims, etc., every few years.)
- What If Lighter? (Like new railroad cars which weigh no more than trailers.)

- Streamline? (Like tank-type vacuum cleaners.)
- Condense? (Like full sized umbrellas that fit into purses.)
- Eliminate? (Like tires without tubes.)

SUBSTITUTE?
- Other Parts? (Like fluid drive instead of gears on cars.)
- Materials? (Like argon instead of a vacuum in electric light bulbs.)
- Other Processes? (Like stamping instead of casting.)
- Other Power? (Like using air to run windshield wipers.)
- Other Way? (Like the airlift that saved Berlin.)

REARRANGE?
- Change Patterns? (Like one way streets.)
- Revise Layout? (Like new arrangements in department stores.)
- After Sequence? (Like storytelling in the movies with flashbacks.)
- Transpose Cause and Effect? (Like doctors do in making diagnoses.)
- Repackage? (Like popcorn that comes in its own microwave bag.)
- Regroup? (Like new defensive systems in football.)

REVERSE?
- Transpose? (Like putting the engine in the rear of the bus.)
- Down Instead of Up? (Like the furrier who attaches his labels upside down so it can be read when the coat is over a chair.)
- Switch Roles? (Like films about female executives with male secretaries.)
- Up Instead of Down? (Like dining room lights which throw a beam upward from the floor to a reflector on the ceiling.)
- Do the Opposite? (Like Howe, who perfected the sewing machine by designing a needle with the hole at the bottom instead of at the top.)

COMBINE?
- How About Alloys? (Like the newest mixes of synthetic fibers.)
- What Old Ideas Could Be Merged? (Like window washers which combine a brush with a built in hose.)
- Ensembles? (Like shirts with neckties and handkerchiefs to match.)
- Book Appeals Together? (Like drugstores selling razor blades to those who ask for shaving cream.)
- Combine Purposes? (Like Benjamin Franklin did when he got tired of switching glasses and invented bifocals.)

Example #2: A Checklist For Headings and Items to Include in a Management Proposal by Robert H. Vaughn
Note: This can be used in conjunction with the format suggested in Chapter Seven of this book.

• Does it need to be in writing, or will an oral presentation do?

• Does the proposal look inviting, i.e., is it neatly presented, free of errors, etc.?

• Is a specific format required? If not, the following headings might be appropriate:

___ Reference to earlier association. (If you've had previous favorable contact with the person or group receiving the proposal, you may want to mention this.)

___ Subject and purpose of proposal. (State clearly and early what you want to change and why it needs to be changed. If the idea would be categorically thrown out, you may need to build up to it. That usually takes too much of the reader's time, however.)

___ Definition of the problem. (Any change should be based on a need. What is your idea in response to?)

___ Background. (Details on how the problem developed may be appropriate.)

___ Need for a solution. (What will happen if no changes are made? When possible tie this to specific dollar amounts, market share, time, etc.)

___ Benefits. (Specifically, what improvements will occur as a result of your idea?)

___ Feasibility. (How practical is the suggestion? What would limit it?)

___ Scope. (Where would this idea apply? One place or many? How widespread would the effects of the change be? Where should the decision be made?)

___ Methods. (How will the proposal be implemented?)

___ Task breakdown. (What, specifically, must be done to make the change happen?)

___ Schedule. (What time frame is required for the change to be implemented?)

___ Facilities. (What facilities will be involved or required?)

___ Experience. (Do you personally have any experience in this? Can you cite examples of where it's been tried before? Who else inside or outside the organization might be able to help?)

___ Personnel. (How many people will the change involve? Who? In what way?)

___ References. (Are there any articles, books, persons, etc., which you can cite in support of the ideas? Remember to include other persons in the organization who have contributed to or already approved of the ideas you're presenting.)

____ Likelihood of success. (No change is perfect. What could keep it from happening? How will you deal with that, or what are the possible consequences? While you may want to play these down, omitting them may be hazardous to your credibility.)

____ Products. (What new reports, new forms, new physical items, new procedures, or whatever, will result from implementing the change?)

____ Cost. (What will it probably cost, and how did you determine that? Remember that kinds of costs , e.g., personnel versus capital equipment, are important distinctions in some organizations.)

____ Appendix. (Include any back up charts, computations, survey data, references, lists, or other items which, while necessary for the decision, would interrupt the flow of the proposal if included in the body of it.)

____ Urge to action. (Summarize, ask for a decision, set a deadline, offer further information, etc.)

Remember: Not all of these will always be appropriate. Pick and choose the ones needed to sell your idea. Several of these might be covered in one sentence, while others might need a paragraph or a whole section each. ***Refer to Chapter 7 which discusses this approach in detail.***

Tool #8: Attribute Listing

Overview:

Attribute listing is a means to evaluate and improve physical items. While it can be used with abstract concepts, it's more difficult. Attribute listing is based on the premise that we think about parts differently than we think about wholes. This tool can be used by either an individual or a group. If done by a group, it can be used in combination with brainstorming concepts (Tool #5).

The phrase, "You can't see the forest for the trees," fits here. This technique is designed to force you to look at both the trees and the forest. It can help you overcome perception problems which block creativity.

The "divide to conquer" process has its roots in Frederick Taylor's application of the scientific method to the study of production. He didn't try to improve the process of coal shoveling — he improved its components; an improvement in the whole process flowed from those changes.

Knowledge or Input Required:

It probably helps to have the physical item available for reference.

Results or Data Output Provided:

A listing of possible uses for an item, possible variations on an item, possible sources for components, etc. is generated as a result of Attribute Listing. These then can be evaluated against other ideas, possibly using the MIT checklist (see Tool #7) or some other tool.

Step by Step Instructions:

Step #1: Mentally and perhaps physically break the object or concept with which you're trying to be creative into its component parts. Instead of thinking about a lawn mower, for example, think about the motor, housing, blade, drive system, handle, etc.

Step #2: Look at each part separately. Ask yourself questions such as: What can you do with each part? How can you change it? What possible problems exist? Etc.

An extensive list of attributes, i.e. ways in which you could physically analyze an object, includes:

Size?	Weight?	Height?	Width?
Volume?	Shape?	Location?	Position?
Arrangement?	Strength?	Composition?	Ingredients?
Hardness?	Color?	Psychological factors?	Crystalline Structure?
Stability?	Adhesion?	Heat properties?	Energy & Power?
Ductility?	Time Properties?		

You may find a number of these terms don't apply to any given component you're analyzing. If so, just ignore them.

An extensive list of questions you can ask yourself about how to change each component can be found in the M.I.T. Checklist (see pages 119–121).

Example:

Your company manufactures greeting cards. You've been assigned to find some ways to cut costs in production. You might analyze the greeting card in the following fashion:
- Size – smaller or more standardized sizes of cards
- Weight – lighter or heavier materials that might work better
- Color – fewer stocks of paper or ink; expand black & white

- Shape – fewer special cut dies or embossments
- Composition – use a less expensive paper or a plastic material
- Etc.

You can see how using a physical attribute list might help you create ideas on how to reduce costs. It's also appropriate to examine other factors of production besides the product itself. Additionally, anything else which adds cost to the product should be fair game for consideration. For example, such things as economies of scale, other types of equipment, using cheaper labor, different distribution channels, pricing policies, etc., all will influence the net profits the company receives.

Tool #9: Morphological Analyses

Overview:

Literally, the name means "analysis of structure." This tool gives you a process to analyze the structure of a decision or problem. This means you break it into its major component parts. Once the structure is analyzed, forced relationship techniques are used in order to produce extensive combinations of ideas.

How many parts should the problem be divided into? A table of four variables with ten choices each would result in 10,000 combinations. It quickly becomes apparent why limiting the choices and variables is necessary, since you must decide on the merits of each combination individually. Think, for example, of a computer program designed to come up with passwords. If you have 26 letters and ten digits (ignoring symbols for the moment), a six-space password with options from "AAAAAA" to "000000" would have 1,947,792 possible combinations. (See the appendix if you want to know how that number was calculated.)

You may already have noticed that the tool name includes the word "analysis." Yes, this tool can also be used to analyze rather than create. The second example provides a model which can be used to analyze an engineering project.

Knowledge or Input Required:

You must know the component parts of a decision to be made or problem to be solved. You might use attribute listing or cause effect analysis to determine components, though they may be somewhat obvious.

Results or Data Output Provided:

This technique creates dozens to thousands of combinations of ideas which can then be analyzed for applicability. It forces you to put things together in ways you might never have considered without using this process.

Step by Step Instructions:

Step 1: Define the issue on which you need to make a decision or the problem to solve.

Step 2: List each of the component parts (independent variables) of the issue or problem. Three to five variables are manageable; fewer make the tool useless and more make it quite cumbersome.

Step 3: Under each of the component parts, list a number of possible choices. 3 to 15 are realistically manageable. Each part does not need the same number of choices. For both steps 2 & 3, then, a certain amount of pre-screening in needed.

Step 4: Develop your options for final evaluation by listing all possible combinations of choices under the parts.

Examples:
Example #1: The Advertising Campaign

You have been hired to advertise a candy store. The component parts or variables could be (1) The occasion for the advertising; (2) The type of prospects; and (3) The medium or method of reaching the audience. For each of these, you've chosen certain options which might be practical. These are shown in the following table.

After building the table, you begin forcing relationships & see if they make sense. Work through it on a 1-1-1; 1-1-2; 1-1-3; 1-1-4; 1-1-x; 1-2-1; 1-2-2; etc. basis. The above example of three variables and six choices would produce 216 possible combinations (computed by 6x6x6=216).

Occasion	Prospect	Medium
Valentine's Day	Children	Radio spot
Mother's Day	Lovers	Parking lot flyers
Easter	Parents	Newspaper ad
Sweetest Day	Executives	Airport display
Halloween	Teachers	Cable TV spot
Birthdays	Senior Citizens	Direct mail

Some of the resulting combinations might be ridiculous (Halloween advertised to Executives through Parking Lot Flyers is probably not a good option), but the process forces you to at least consider the possibilities.

Example #2: The Comprehensive Morphology

This "generic model" was created to show how a rather complete analysis of an engineering project can be handled. Following the analysis of the project, you can use it as a basis for assigning tasks and scheduling.

You will undoubtedly find a number of items which don't apply to any given problem or project you're analyzing. Simply cross out those that don't apply and use the other ones. For example, let's say you're trying to design a computer system for your office. The attributes that probably could be crossed off include: ductility, crystalline structure, adhesion, hardness, ingredients, and others. Those which remain may provide you a good tool (structure) for decision making and/or problem solving.

Attribute Checklist	Possible Action	Project Management
Size	Other Use?	Who?
Height	Adapt?	What?
Width	Modify?	When?
Weight	Magnify?	Where?
Volume	Duplicate?	Why?
Shape	Multiply?	How?
Position	Exaggerate?	How much?
Location	Add to?	How often?
Arrangement	Maximize?	
Strength	Minimize?	
Composition	Substitute?	
Ingredients	Rearrange?	
Hardness	Reverse?	
Color	Invert?	
Psychological	Combine?	
Stability	Inside out?	
Adhesion	Omit?	
Heat properties	Take apart?	
Crystalline Structure	Synthesize?	
Ductility		
Time Properties		
Energy & Power		

Tool #10: Catalog Technique

Overview:

The catalog technique is a means to come up with additional options and alternatives to any decision making or problem solving issue. It allows the decision maker to tap into already created lists, some of which will probably expand in unexpected ways.

Note that what is being called a "catalog" may come in a variety of guises: directories, classified section of a magazine or newspaper, databases, etc., as well as the more traditional meaning of the word. If the problem or decision is a major one, it will be worth the time to visit your local library or contact an individual or organization which specializes in research. Some places to start looking to find the catalogs you need include:

Professional or industry associations in the area you're researching. For example, if you need a film about training skills, contact organizations such as The American Society for Training and Development, National Education Association, and so on. Your library probably has a Directory of Associations which can give you some leads.

Commercial Research Data Base Sources which can provide names of companies and agencies which might be useful by use of several keywords. The most obvious sources for most people these days, ***Google©, Yahoo!©, Ask.com©, and the myriad of other search engines available on the world-wide web*** are some of the better known "layman" sources of tapping into the more specific data base providers.

Industrial Directories such as Moody's or Dun and Bradstreet, or many others your librarian can list. You can then contact these listed companies for product or service details which might help your decision.

Knowledge or Input Required:

Where to find appropriate catalogs. This simple phrase hides a great deal of complexity. *Finding the appropriate catalogs* is the key — the only key — to making this tool work effectively for you. An effective "catalog" allows you to get the ideas you need. Not having a catalog, of course, means you can't use the tool.

Results or Data Output Provided:

A listing of alternatives is generated which can then be evaluated against decision making criteria.

Step by Step Instructions:

There's no need to over complicate this. All we're talking about is using existing "catalog" or search engine types of resources to come up with ideas. Basically, this is simple research. The key is to find the right catalogs or databases to be useful. *Recall the comments from Chapter Five (page 56) regarding the issues of volume and credibility when using computer-based resources.*

Step 1: Find an appropriate catalog or database for the problem you face, and review the contents.

Example:

Problem	Typical "Catalog"
What to buy for Uncle Harry's birthday	Penney's, Ace Hardware, Victoria's Secret
How to landscape & decorate the yard	Seed & nursery catalog; Yellow Pages
How to connect an additional printer	Computer hardware catalog
Joining two awkward machine components	Specialty tool catalog
Finding clients for an Ad Agency	City Directory
What to serve special guests	A Cookbook
How to entertain kids	Toy store, list of museums, Movie or video listing
How to get a product to Kansas	Wizard of Oz® Spells & Storms Catalog

The example above suggests problems which can be solved more creatively by using a catalog as a resource for ideas. We often find new or creative solutions which we didn't know existed.

Tool #11: Artificial Intelligence & its Subcategory: Expert Systems

Note: This is the only tool in the book which requires a computer, though many other tools such as queuing are aided by a computer.

Overview:

Artificial Intelligence ("A.I.") is a computer-supported, logic-based system to help decision making. It gives the appearance of human-like reasoning for problems ordinarily requiring an expert.

A.I. software programs come in many forms. Some are designed for and dedicated to a particular process such as the mixing of chemicals or narrowing down leads for a criminal investigation. Some are user software programs which allow anyone to design their own A.I. applications. One general category of A.I. is "expert systems" in which the user answers questions and the computer then generates recommendations in the same manner one might ask questions of and get advice from an expert.

A.I. programs are not as widely known as other software categories such as word processing, spreadsheets or databases. Their importance in management decision making is growing rapidly as user-friendly software is developed which can be adapted to a variety of situations. Some of the programs will operate in the background of other programs (as Windows does, for example) so the user can interact and call other programs as necessary.

Several major periodicals and probably hundreds of books are available on the subject. Over 400 different companies produce some form of A.I. software, including some which are as easy to use as simple word processors and cost well under $1,000.

An example of artificial intelligence systems with which most of you are probably familiar is the so-called "wizard" programs used to solve installation or operational problems related to computer software. Microsoft Office's dancing paper clip is an artificial intelligence program (though you are warned not to judge the entire genre by that example). A medical diagnosis AI program might even learn from its mistakes and successes. Based on input from the doctor regarding symptoms, medical test results, etc., it might provide diagnoses and suggested remedies. If information is later input regarding the accuracy of the diagnosis or success of the proposed remedy, this information is incorporated into the program for use in developing future answers.

Knowledge or Input Required:

A computer and artificial intelligence software designed to aid decision making in the area under discussion. You must know how to use the software and hardware. The software will ask specific questions related to the problem or decision for which you will need answers.

Expert systems can be used when:

The domain (i.e., the rules, limits, standards, etc.) is well-defined and stable.

The solution to the problem or decision is not dependent on just common sense.

The same decision must be made frequently with different information, as in a diagnosis of illness or recommendation of a college schedule or pricing of an insurance policy. These things are done frequently by doctors, academic advisors, and insurance agents, but for different patients, students and customers.

An expert is available to develop the knowledge base (facts and rules) which asks the questions, and design the inference questions which are used to evaluate input by the users.

Results or Data Output Provided:

The typical output is a prioritized list of options or recommendations.

Step by Step Instructions:

This will vary with the software design. Follow the screen or documentation instructions for the program.

Example:

Expert System for use in Deciding on an Automobile to Purchase

Input required into the program: Automobiles available, prices of each, handling characteristics, comfort & safety ratings of each, etc. Once programmed, a simple A.I. expert system interaction might operate in the following manner:

The **bold** questions would be asked by the computer, and the *italics* represent a user's possible responses. The screen would offer a series of questions to which the user chooses a response.

What product purchase are you considering?
automobile   van   pickup truck   other

What maximum price would you spend for this vehicle?
enter a dollar value:

Will you be doing more city or highway driving?
highway   city   mixed

Is comfort or economy a higher priority?
economy   comfort

Is safety a high, medium or low priority?
high   medium   low

Are there any brand names you would not consider?
enter one or more

Thank you for your input. The computer is now ready to print a list of options prioritized by price for your further consideration. You may then request further specifications on any of these automobiles.

Other Selected Creativity Tools

The subject of creativity-enhancing techniques is broad and varied. The previous seven tools and their subcategories are just a sampling of the better known ones. The interested reader is referred to the bibliography. A book which discusses these ideas at a similar level to this text is *Creative Thinking in the Decision and Management Sciences* by James R. Evans.

Synectics, from the Greek word meaning to join together different elements, is a technique developed by William J. J. Gordon of Arthur D. Little, Inc., in the 1950's. He noticed that when a particularly novel idea appeared, it was usually expressed as an analogy or metaphor. The process requires a group to attack an underlying concept of the problem, rather than the problem itself. Fantasies can be used with this, as well as other techniques.

Dream Diaries can be used to tap into the subconscious way our minds organize and process information. Many of the great inventions were, literally, "dreamed up" by their originators. Most people forget dreams and ideas quickly, so learning to record ideas quickly is useful. Encourage dreams by self-suggestions, i.e., telling yourself that you'd like to work on a problem while you sleep or meditate.

Relaxation Techniques, often associated with relieving stress, can also remove barriers to creativity. Meditation, biofeedback, and others can be useful when properly handled. More detail on these may be found in other books listed in the bibliography.

Guided Fantasies require a leader to develop a simple scenario which the individual's (or group's) unconscious can use to flesh out details. They usually begin and return in reality, but dabble in fantasy in a way that the follower (s) can construct their own methodology for dealing with issues presented by the leader. There is some similarity with this technique and dreaming, except that this is externally guided.

Free Associating is a process in which you "turn your mind loose" to let one idea lead to another to another to another. This has some of the characteristics of brainstorming, in that ideas tend to flow. It can also be done in a group, and is best done either with a tape recorder or some other way of marking the path for retracing later.

Doodling is graphical free associating. It could be useful for creating ideas which are visual in nature such as a corporate logo or other free form design. Some computer programs are ideal for assisting in this.

Delphi Technique is a process of decision making by using cycles of independent decisions made by experts who do not interact with each other. In a way, it could be thought of as brainstorming by long distance. The leader (person who poses the question) gets responses from each expert, summarizes them, then sends the summaries back to the group for further refinement. This may be repeated several times. It gets some of the groupthink or follow the leader problems out of the brainstorming process. An example of a Delphi Technique series of questions is included on the computer support disk which came with this book.

All of these techniques (tools) and many others are designed to help us become more creative — to overcome those barriers that Adams talks about.

Summary

This chapter provided an overview and directions for applying each of seven tool categories, and briefly mentioned a number of others, all of which are designed to help increase our creativity and innovativeness.

Brainstorming is a well-known process which encourages a quantity of ideas by tapping into the collective resources of a group. Several variations of that technique were discussed, along with some other techniques which can be used by groups include cause-effect analysis, attribute listing and morphological analysis.

Individual creativity techniques include some of those already mentioned which can be done with or without a group, along with checklists, catalogs, artificial intelligence, free associating and others.

Study Questions:

1. Describe some of the advantages and disadvantages of traditional brainstorming.
2. How can the Gordon technique and Delphi technique be used to avoid some of the problems of traditional brainstorming?
3. Name several different approaches to cause-effect analysis.
4. What is a potential problem with both the checklist and catalog techniques?
5. Between attribute listing and morphological analysis, which one forces combinations and which forces separations?
6. What makes artificial intelligence more complicated to use than the other techniques described in this textbook?

Exercise:

Choose which techniques would work well and not work well with the following problems or decisions.

Techniques:

A - Brainstorming	E - Morphological Analyses
B - Cause Effect Analyses	F - Catalog Technique
C - Checklists	G - Artificial Intelligence
D - Attribute Listing	H - Other

Problems or Decisions:

1. Deciding between two insurance proposals.
2. Figuring out why a copier keeps jamming.
3. Planning a wedding.
4. Choosing a color of paint for the office.
5. Getting rescued from a desert island.

CHAPTER 10

Tools to Compare and Evaluate Options

"Did you ever have to make up your mind? Say 'yes' to one and leave the other behind? It's not often easy; it's not often kind. Did you ever have to make up your mind?"

– The Lovin' Spoonful

Chapter Objectives:

This chapter is designed to enable the reader to ....
- Understand when and how to use decision matrices.
- Understand when and how to use expected value analyses.
- Understand when and how to use decision trees.
- Understand when and how to use decomposition trees.
- Understand when and how to use scatter diagrams.
- Understand when and how to use economic order quantity analysis.
- Understand when and how to use break even analysis.
- Understand when and how to use queuing analysis.
- Be aware of a variety of other analytical tools which might be used.

The tools in Chapter 10 relate to the concepts covered in Chapter 5.

The tools described in this chapter all can be used to compare options once a list of possible choices or possible causes has been created. The information on data gathering in Chapter Five is relevant here. Your decisions using these tools are only as good as the data you put into the tool. The "GISGO" principle applies: Garbage In, Scientific Garbage Out.

The tools in this chapter include:

DECISION MATRICES are a generic tool which can be used as an aid to help structure data for nearly any type of a decision.

EXPECTED VALUES ANALYSIS takes the simple Decision Matrix model and allows quantification to help analyze among various options associated with such things as work output, inventory mixes, investment portfolios, etc.

DECISION TREES are a concept usually credited to Victor Vroom, who is also known for his motivation theory. Decision trees represent a stream of consciousness type of analysis, taking each possible outcome as a "branch" off the decision. Each of these can be analyzed for probability and net result.

DECOMPOSITION TREES, also called Value Trees, are useful visual techniques for dissecting or decomposing a large concept into its component parts in order to determine its makeup and / or assign weights or priorities to its elements.

SCATTER DIAGRAMS are useful (as discussed in Chapter Five) to help determine the relationship (or absence of) between sets of data. They can also be effectively employed as concurrent or even forward looking control techniques, as described in Chapters Two and Eight.

ECONOMIC ORDER QUANTITY ANALYSIS, also called Economic Lot Size, applies to inventory and purchasing decisions, and helps determine the most cost effective quantity to order. It can also be used for other types of decisions where countervailing costs exist.

BREAK EVEN ANALYSIS is a way of determining whether or not it will be profitable to undertake a project of some sort. While normally associated with manufacturing, it can also apply to services, rent or buy decisions, inventory, etc.

QUEUING ANALYSIS is a technique which can be applied to a number of decision making scenarios. It is presented in a limited format here, although access to a computer program or understanding of statistics could make it more flexible.

Several other tools will be briefly covered in the final section, but not discussed in any detail. Very seldom will any of these tools give you an absolute answer. They will provide information to *help* your decision making, but the final decision usually involves a certain amount of risk.

Tool # 12: Decision Matrix

Overview:

The decision matrix is a deductive tool for general decision making among options of various types. The overall purpose of using a Decision Matrix is to provide a structure to compare options that are not necessarily directly comparable, due to their complexity. It forces the analyst to consider each option, one criteria at a time, therefore structuring his or her thoughts rationally. This is particularly helpful in the often occurring situation where each option has some good and some bad points, and therefore no clear choice emerges.

Typical decisions which might be aided by a decision matrix are: where to go on vacation, which new car to buy, where to open up a branch office, which applicant to hire for a job opening, or any other decision among complex alternatives.

The decision matrix can be developed in several forms. We will introduce them from the simplest to more complex. The first is extremely simple, employing only a "yes or no" judgment. Next, we add scaling, then weighting to the process.

Knowledge or Input Required:

To use a decision matrix, the analyst must know: (1) The options available, (2) Any specific facts which are important in the consideration of these options – i.e., what are the relevant criteria, and (3) The relative importance of each of these criteria.

Several points are appropriate to mention to aid the explanations below. First, some terminology: As is the case with spreadsheets, "Row" means items on the horizontal line; "Column" means items on a vertical line. "Cell" is the intersection of a row and a column, and contains one datum or piece of data. This terminology is important to working with any matrix form. Next, if all options being considered are identical (or vary insignificantly) on any criterion, that criterion need not be listed, even if it seems important. Finally, all possible choices must meet minimum standards of acceptability, or they need not be evaluated. Some readers may be familiar with Kepner-Tregoe decision techniques which use a "musts" and "wants" division in their criteria (see the reference in the appendix). The perspective in this book is that if your choice does not meet all the "must" criteria, it should not be listed as a choice under consideration.

Results or Data Output Provided:

The decision matrix generates an imprecise but relative rating number. This number may be adequate to make the final decision, or may be used in subsequent, more objective comparisons of the options under consideration. The higher numbers indicate the more favorable options.

Step by Step Instructions:
For the simplest format.

Step 1: Determine the options you want to consider.

Step 2: List the options across the top of a sheet of paper.

Step 3: Determine and list down the left hand column, major criteria (considerations) which are important to you in making this decision.

Step 4: Place a check mark under each option beside each criterion which exists in the option.

Step 5: Count the check marks; whichever option has the most is the best choice. See Example 1.

Step by Step Instructions:
For an unweighted format.

Steps 1 – 3: Same as above.

Step 4: Choose a relative rating scale – for example, 1-5, with 5 being the best.

- *Note*: It is important to be consistent in the application of the scale. If evaluating possible houses to buy, use the highest rating for the <u>lowest</u> price and for the <u>highest</u> resale value. Sometimes the "best" numbers on one criterion are the low ones, and sometimes they're the high ones. Your scale must reflect that. Also, ties are acceptable.

Step 5: Rate each option on each criteria using the selected scale.

Step 6: Add the numbers for each column. The highest total is the best choice. See Example 2.

Step by Step Instructions:
For a weighted format.

Steps 1 – 5: Same as immediately above.

Step 6: Make another column next to the criteria. In this, rate the significance of each criteria relative to the others on a scale (again, 1-5 is probably adequate). This weights each criterion.

Step 7: Multiply each score from step 5 by the weight in that row.

Step 8: Add the products in each column. Again, the highest total is the best choice. See Examples 3 and 4.

Examples:
Example 1: Unweighted Decision Matrix on Vacation Choices

You are trying to decide where to take a family vacation. You have narrowed it to four possible options: **the Mountains, the Seashore, an Overseas Site, or A Big City.** For the first (simplest) example, you might just list things you'd like to do on a vacation. Following the steps above, you would come up with this matrix.

Based on this, your choice would be to go to the mountains, since it received the greatest number of check marks. Note, also, that since all four options received check marks under "entertainment for spouse & me," that particular criterion had no effect on the outcome, and could have been eliminated.

Example 1: Simple Decision Matrix

Criteria	Mountains	Seashore	Overseas	Big City
Fresh air	✔	✔		
Entertainment for kids		✔	✔	✔
Entertainment for spouse & me	✔	✔	✔	✔
Quiet	✔			
Low cost	✔			
Can work on tan		✔	✔	
Lack of crowds	✔			
Totals	5	4	3	2

In the next decision matrix related to your vacation, you might list the following considerations: **Likely Cost; Travel time required; Relaxation expected; Ease of travel to the site; and Family fun.**

Let's assume your thought process goes like this:

- Mountains: Low cost, but a long drive. It'll be relaxing and no complications about getting there. Your kids hate the idea.
- Seashore: More expensive than the mountains, but closer. It, too, will be relaxing. Drive goes through big cities. Kids approve; spouse is ambivalent.
- Overseas: Expensive, but flying is quick. Tough to relax in unfamiliar surroundings. Need passport, different money, interpreter & guide. Sounds like fun to the family.
- Big city: Expensive, short drive, hectic, but not too complex. Lots of museums and excitement.

The resulting decision matrix is shown below. In this case, you don't have a clear winner since the best two columns have equal scores. You can at least eliminate two of the options (overseas and big city), then go back and add some other criteria — or just flip a coin.

Example 2: Using a 1-5 scale for each item

Criteria	Mountains	Seashore	Overseas	Big City
Likely Cost	5	3	1	2
Travel Time	2	4	4	3
Relaxation	5	5	2	3
Ease of Travel	5	3	1	2
Family Fun	1	3	5	5
Total Points	18	18	13	15

Example 3: Weighted Decision Matrix on Vacation Choices

In all probability, however, your criteria are not of equal importance to you. The matrix on the following page adds a criterion weighting scale of 1 to 10, which takes that into account. This gives cost the major impact on the decision, with ease of travel and relaxation as the two least important.

Your preference would be for the choice which received the greatest number of points, so this would eliminate an overseas or big city vacation. In this case, that the seashore is best and the mountains a close second.

Example 3: Weighted decision matrix

Criteria	Weight	Mountains	Seashore	Overseas	Big City
Likely Cost	9	5	4	1	2
Travel Time	6	2	4	4	3
Relaxation	4	5	5	2	3
Ease of Travel	4	5	3	1	2
Family Fun	7	1	3	5	5
Total Points		104	113	71	91

Example 4: Weighted Decision Matrix on Relocation Choices

You must decide where to open the new eastern states sales office for your company which is based in San Francisco. Preliminary information on your market suggests Atlanta, Cleveland and Washington as possible sites. You set up your decision matrix with these cities listed across the top.

Next, you determine the criteria which should influence your decision. What these should be, of course, will depend on the nature of your product and support needed by the sales staff. For example, if salespeople call in from wherever they're based and seldom visit the office, the relative cost of living is of minor concern. Conversely, if most of the employees actually work in the sales office, then it is more important.

Here are some criteria which might apply:
- Percent of potential market which is closer to option cities than to San Francisco. Highest percentage gets the most points.
- Operating cost for planned office (lease costs, taxes, prevailing wages, etc.). Remember: lowest cost gets the most points in this case.
- Airport efficiency in meeting customer and employee needs.
- Acceptability to employees (cost of living, weather, cultural and recreation, etc.) One catalog you might use to get this information is the annual Places Rated Almanac which provides city by city scores that could be used for this analysis.
- And so on.

Shown on the next page is a potential matrix for this decision.

The obvious choice for the eastern states sales office is Cleveland.

Example 4: Relocation Decision Matrix

Criteria	Weight	Atlanta	Cleveland	Washington DC
Market Proximity	3	5	7	8
Office Cost	2	6	9	2
Airport	1	5	4	4
Places Rated Score	4	6	8	7
Weighted Score		65	75	60

Tool #13: Expected Value Computation

Overview:

This tool is designed to help determine the ***expected value*** of a transaction. Expected Values are index numbers useful as a basis for comparison of alternatives. The expected value computation uses a combination of the decision matrix (Tool #12) and probabilities (see Chapter Five and the appendix).

The basic difference between this tool and the decision matrix is that the decision matrix uses check marks or some relative scale (such as 1 to 5) to evaluate each criterion, while entries in the expected value matrix are real numbers representing actual or projected outcomes from each alternative under the various conditions.

Knowledge or Input Required:

Group input may be helpful to predict probabilities or determine options. To create an expected value matrix, the analyst must know: (1) What alternatives are available to choose (the rows), (2) The likely conditions under which these alternatives will be operating (the columns), and (3) The predicted result for each alternative under each condition (to be entered in the cells). Also, an expected probability for each condition will help refine the analysis.

Results or Data Output Provided:

Computing the expected value of various alternative courses of action will provide a basis for comparison of each to the others. While the actual outcome is unlikely to be exactly as computed, a relative likelihood of profit or value can be established among the alternatives under various conditions. The result of the computation is an index number for each alternative.

Step by Step Instructions:

Step 1: List vertically the various options being considered.

Step 2: List horizontally across the top the various conditions which might occur to affect the outcome.

Step 3: Determine what the result is likely to be for each of the options under each of the conditions specified. Enter this index number in the appropriate cell in the matrix.

Step 4a: If the conditions are equally likely, compute the expected value by simply taking the average of the rates for each of the options.

Step 4b: If the conditions are not equally likely, this changes the analysis. Predict the likelihood of each condition, then compute the Expected Value by weighting the table in a manner similar to that described for the Decision Matrix.

Examples:

Example 1: Unweighted Expected Value Matrix on Investments

In this example, a choice is to be made among three different investment options. They are shown in the matrix as A, B, and C. These investment options include a variety of stock, bond, commodity, and other options, and will perform differently based on different economic conditions.

The possible economic conditions are: Inflation, Depression and Recession.

A financial advisor can project the likely response of each of these portfolios to each economic condition. She has provided her estimate of what annual payout will result for each $100 you invest. These are shown in the matrix. For example, under inflation, Policy A will pay $16 for each $100 invested, but only $6 in the case of a recession. The other numbers are also based on the payout for $100 for the policy in that row and the economic condition in that column.

If the likelihood of each economic condition is equal, then the expected value can be computed by simply adding numbers in each row and dividing by three, as shown in the example. Policy A would be the best choice, in this case, since it has the highest expected value. Policy C would be second, and B last.

Unweighted Expected Value Matrix

Policy	Inflation	Depression	Recession	Expected Value	Computed by
A	16	11	6	11	(16+11+6)/3
B	8	11	-1	6	(8+11-1)/3
C	4	14	9	9	(4+14+9)/3

Essentially, what this means is that if this investment was made over and over and over, it would result in an average return of 11, 6 or 9 dollars per hundred in the long run. But it's only this simple if all possibilities are equal. That seldom happens in real life. This leads us on to example number two.

Example 2: Weighted Expected Value Matrix on Investments

Let's say that there is a 70% chance for Recession, a 20% chance for Inflation and a 10% chance for Depression (they add up to 100%, of course). Now the table can be modified to look like this:

Now Policy C looks just as good as Policy A. Of course it's impossible to know exactly what will happen on any one occasion, but this data is input to the decision.

Another question to ask is: "How much would additional information or some action to insure one situation happening over another be worth?"

In example 2, what would an investor be willing to pay a politician to insure that an inflation occurred? [Or pay another expert for their opinion?] If the investor knew it was going to be inflation, they would certainly choose Policy A over Policy C. What do you think? They might choose A anyhow (50/50 chance). Is it worth $5 per $100 to know what it'll be? There's a further discussion of this question in the Appendix.

Weighted Expected Value Matrix

Policy	Inflation	Depression	Recession	Expected Value	Computed by
Probability =	20%	10%	70%	100%	
A	16	11	6	8.5	(.2)16+(.1)11+(.7)6=8.5
B	8	11	-1	2	(.2)8+(.1)11+(.7)(-1)=2.0
C	4	14	9	8.5	(.2)4+(.1)14+(.7)9=8.5

Tool #14: Decision Trees

Overview:

Decision trees help to visualize and follow to conclusion the logic of decisions and their consequences based on chance events subsequent to the decision. As such, they provide a basis for either subjective or objective comparison of options. They essentially represent the same data as a multi-level expected value matrix.

Even if you don't get to the stage of making computations and assigning probabilities, just listing the options and potential results can be helpful in structuring your thinking about the decision.

Knowledge or Input Required:

Options available for the decision and the likelihood and value of subsequent events.

Results or Data Output Provided:

A graphic "tree" shows the options, providing a map to all projected possible outcomes. When combined with probabilities or expected values, a quantitative projection of results is possible.

Step by Step Instructions:

Step 1: Starting at the left of the page, list your decision to be made as the "trunk" of the tree, and the options as the first "limbs."

Step 2: From each of the limbs, divide out into projected results (branches) from a future chance event under different conditions (same set of conditions for each limb). Repeat this step one or two more times, if appropriate to consider more than one future chance event.

Step 3: Assign probabilities to the chance events and a dollar value (or other quantifiable value) to the expected implementation cost and resulting profit under those events.

Step 4: Multiply out the probabilities and values, and add them up for each initial option. The best option is the one with the most favorable total expected value.

Example:

This company must make a decision about how to produce of a new line of products. The three options being considered are a permanent tooling investment, a temporary tooling investment or subcontracting the project. The initial tree looks like this:

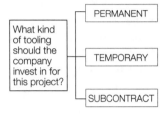

The options which may happen with any of the above choices will be defined as "success," "partial success," or "failure." The expanded Decision Tree showing this is below.

Now we'll assign a probability to each of the conditions and a cost and projected profit to each of the options. Let's say that the Permanent tooling will cost $1 million, the Temporary $400,000, and the Subcontract requires a guarantee of $150,000. These figures are completed in the next part of the example.

Further, suppose that if the product is a SUCCESS, the return, if we use permanent tooling, is expected to be $425,000 a year for five years. The return on temporary tooling will be $190,000 per year for three years, and the return from subcontracting will be $80,000 a year for five years. If the product is a PARTIAL SUCCESS, we'll make 40% of the total success figures above. If it's a FAILURE, we lose our investment plus 10% opportunity cost. Now, give it a 40% chance of success and a 30% chance of being at least a partial success.

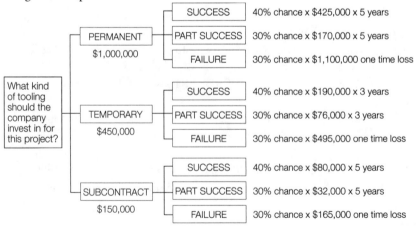

Finally, compute the expected return on each of the three options, given the assumptions we've presented above. To do this, multiply the figures shown beside each branch in the tree above, add them for the three possibilities for each initial choice option, then subtract the required initial investment. This gives you the Expected Value for each of the choices. This is shown following as "Net" figures. (NOTE: If you skipped the previous tool, you need to go back to it to understand the concept of expected values.) The highest numbers generally represent the best choices. The tree on the next page indicates the best choice to be permanent tooling, given our criteria.

If the company can't get the financing for the $1,000,000 investment, the next best choice is to subcontract, rather than go with temporary tooling. The company can anticipate making a profit in any of the three choices. There is, of course, a 30% chance of failure in any of the options.

If we're looking for return on investment rather than total profit, the best bet is subcontracting. This is most likely to give us the highest return on the amount invested, but it doesn't give us the highest total profit.

All of this depends on the accuracy of our estimates of cost and probability of success. Good data on those items is important. The actual possible outcomes under the conditions described above would range from a profit of $1,125,000 to a loss of $1,100,000.

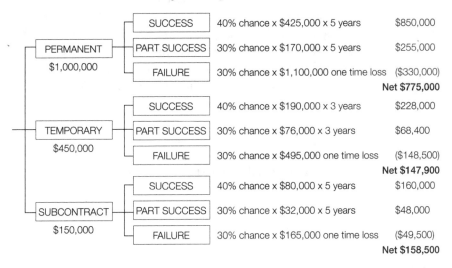

It is also possible to do the above tree in a matrix form (see below). The table loses the detail of how the numbers were computed, so the better choice might be to use a spreadsheet program. The principles are the same in all methods. A complete matrix to show all the details would need to be multi-dimensional to account for 3 tooling options, 3 levels of success, the probability for each level, the term (years) for each option and the cost for each option. Because of all this detail, a tree is easier to follow than a complex matrix.

Weighted Expected Value Matrix on Tooling Decision (in thousands)				
Choice	Total Success	Partial Success	Failure	Expected Value
Probability =	40%	30%	30%	
Permanent	$850	$225	-$330	$775.0
Temporary	$228	$68.4	-$148.5	$147.9
Subcontract	$160	$48	-$49.5	$158.5

Tool #15: Decomposition Trees *(Also called Value Trees)*

Overview:

Decomposition trees are a visual aid to understanding the parts which make-up a whole. The trees essentially look like traditional organization charts. Their purpose is to help in the "decomposition" or breaking up a larger item into its components. They could be used for a variety of decision making or problem solving needs such as to analyze a budget, review staffing in an organization, or help with a job analysis by a human resources specialist to determine what tasks an individual performs in a job. The results might also be used in the development of a Pareto Analysis (see Chapter Five).

Knowledge or Input Required:

The manager or analyst must understand whatever "whole" is being decomposed, and have appropriate information available about the various parts.

Results or Data Output:

The output is a visual "tree" with relative values indicated for each part.

Step by Step Instructions:

Step 1: On the top line of a sheet of paper, list the unit to be analyzed (the entire budget, organization, job, etc.)

Step 2: Break the whole out into its major parts, and indicate the appropriate value for each part beside it on the next lower line. The value might be in percentages or in real numbers. If percentages, they should add to 100%. If real numbers, they should add to the same totals on each line.

Step 3: Continue repeating this process until you have reached the level necessary for whatever analysis you are conducting.

Examples:

Example 1: Analysis of the Company Budget

As part of the data collection to plan for the company's budget for next year, you have decided to use a decomposition tree to display the current budget. You will decompose the current budget allocation according to the organization structure. The resulting tree is shown below.

This then provides a basis for the manager or analyst to ask questions and effectively compare across the organization. Is it appropriate, for example, for the Sales Department to have nearly six times the budget of the Human Resource Department?

Note that each level adds to $1,000,000 or 100%.

Example 1: Company Budget Decomposition

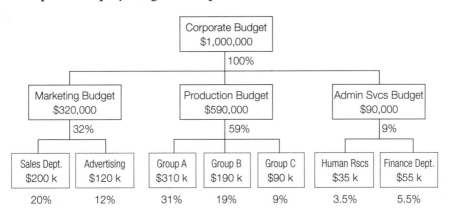

Example 2: Analysis of a Receptionist Position

The first division of the job is into four main tasks, then each is subdivided into two or three sub tasks. Again, each of the levels adds up to 100%. This concept will be used again in Chapter Eleven.

Example 2: Receptionist Workday

Receptionist			
Telephone 24%	Greet Visitors 28%	Typing Overflow 32%	Mail 16%
Take orders 12% Inquiries 8% Other 4%	Keep Log 8% Notify Employees 5% Provide Information 15%	Memos 18% Reports 10% Other 4%	Prep Outgoing 11% Sort Incoming 5%

Tool #16: Scatter Diagrams

Overview:

Scatter diagrams visually indicate relationships or absence of them between two sets of data. They were introduced briefly in Chapter Five under the heading "Correlation." Scatter Diagrams compare and show the relationship of one factor to another such as:

height & weight   price & sales

work done & people working   accidents and age

day of week & customers   and any other pairing of data

Knowledge or Input Required:

To use scatter diagrams, the analyst needs information on the sets of data which are to be compared and, in the case of control charts, what standards are required. A basic understanding of the use of graphing is also necessary.

Results or Data Output:

Scatter diagrams can suggest whether or not a relationship exists between sets of data. For example, does the speed of a conveyor influence the number of defects produced? Does the amount of fertilizer affect the yield of an acre of corn? Is the average personal income level of a city a true indicator of the potential sales of a product? Etc.

Step by Step Instructions:

Step 1: Determine what sets of data need to be compared. Make certain they're appropriately stratified to provide an accurate analysis. For example, if you're comparing productivity of employees compared to the amount of formal training they've received, it would be best to group new employees and experienced employees separately. Otherwise, you'll not be able to analyze whether the productivity is related to training or to experience on the job.

Step 2: On graph paper (or by some other appropriate means), lay out vertical and horizontal axes (yes, that's the plural of axis), and determine which data to scale along which axis. Certain conventions should be observed. For example, time should be shown horizontally, with earliest times at the left. Unconventional scaling interferes with effectively communicating the information to others. Common sense usually works, but if you want more information, you need to find a reference on graphics presentation.

Step 3: Place a dot or other indication ("x", etc.) at the intersection of the coordinates which represent each set of data.

Step 4: Examine the resulting pattern of dots for evidence which suggests or denies the existence of relationships in the data. Statistical measures of the degree of actual relationship can be determined using correlation-regression analysis and other techniques. Again, see the appendix and bibliography for sources of further information.

Examples:

These examples are the same ones shown earlier. (page 64). See the notes which follow.

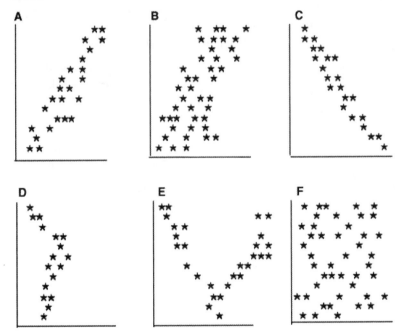

- **A** - <u>Positive Relationship:</u> This scatter diagram gives a pretty good indication that when one of the two data items goes up, the other probably will too. If you could draw a straight line that went through all points, it would be a perfect relationship (100% correlation). That would mean that each move on the vertical axis would have an exactly predictable move along the horizontal axis. For example, if you were buying apples at twenty-five cents each, and plotted the number of apples along the vertical axis and the total price paid along the horizontal, it would be a perfectly straight line between the points.

- **B** - <u>Linear, Positive Loose Relationships:</u> This diagram has the basic elements of A, but it's "looser." That means you can't be as sure of the relationship with small changes in one data set. In statistical terms, the correlation is lower. If you were plotting the height and weight of people, you'd probably get a chart like this. Most people who are 6'4" would weigh more than most who are 4'10". However, you couldn't be sure that someone who's 5'11" weighs more than someone who's 5'9". The looser the relationship, the less you can rely on the data's predictability.

- **C** - <u>Negative Relation:</u> As one piece of data goes up, the other will go down. For example, if you plotted price on the vertical axis and the number sold on the horizontal axis, most products would give a diagram such as this. The higher the price, the fewer sold; the lower the price, the more will sell, other things being equal.

- **D & E** - <u>Non-linear Relationships:</u> Patterns in these diagrams indicate that there probably is some relationship — you can draw a single line that will go fairly near all the points. The line, however, isn't straight. There are statistical formulae to determine the mathematical equation of the line which has the best fit to the dots. This will give you the predicted mathematical relation between the two data sets. (See the appendix for further information.) Frequently the visual or approximate information you get from the diagram is all that is necessary for decision making.

- **F** - <u>No Relationship:</u> If the scatter diagram looks like this, there is no relationship between the data plotted on the vertical (Y) axis and the data plotted on the horizontal (X) axis. They are independent of each other. If one goes up, the other may go up, down, or not change. You can make no judgments from data such as this, except that they're probably not related.

Tool #17: Economic Order Quantity Calculation
(also called Economic Lot Size)

Overview:

This tool is not limited to inventory management, though that is where it may have originated. In the inventory management context, EOQ helps the manager determine the most economical lot size for ordering of stock (parts, supplies, merchandise, etc.). One calculation is necessary for each major inventory item.

In reality, the model may be used anywhere the manager or decision maker is faced with some form of countervailing costs. (Countervailing costs are where one cost goes up as another goes down.) For example, in deciding how often equipment maintenance should be done, there are countervailing costs. One is the cost of excessive down time for the equipment, and the other is the cost of excessive maintenance. See the second example below.

Knowledge or Input Required:

The analyst or decision maker needs to know: (1) Whether or not the stock items or subjects under consideration represent a significant enough cost to warrant the data collection and calculation, and (2) What the various ordering and storage costs are for each of the items to be analyzed.

Results or Data Output Provided:

The EOQ calculation will provide the optimum number of orders per year which should be made to minimize total cost of inventory operations. If dealing with decisions other than inventory, it produces a number which will optimize the balance between countervailing costs.

Step by Step Instructions:

Step 1: Determine which stock item (s) you wish to evaluate with an EOQ Calculation. ***Note:*** Collecting the data will take some time, and the savings on low cost & low volume items probably won't justify the time and effort to compute the EOQ. See the discussion on Pareto Analysis in Chapter Five. As a general rule, if the goods are large or expensive or critical to the process, they should be evaluated.

Step 2: Determine the number of units needed per year and their average cost.

Step 3: Collect information on costs of ordering the item being reviewed. These costs should include:

- The cost of preparing an order (writing the order out or phoning, e-mailing or faxing it, or completing it on-line, and the cost of preparing the check, etc.)
- The cost of receiving the order (administrative time to sign for it, deliver it to stock, open and verify the correct number were received, etc.)
- If there are quantity discounts, minimum order lots, or other changes in price based on the size of the order each time, these must be incorporated.
- The freight cost per item. Does it go down with larger quantities?
- Any other costs are associated with ordering this item for inventory.

Step 4: Collect information on costs of holding the item being reviewed in inventory. These costs should include:

- Space cost per item. How much does it cost to rent/lease the space; how much to heat it, provide electrical support, etc.?
- Tax difference: How much difference does the value of one piece make in the various business taxes?
- Risk cost: how much for insurance? How much chance of loss or obsolescence?
- Interest cost or lost opportunity cost for value of merchandise tied up in inventory.
- Risk of stock out & associated costs.
- Any other costs are associated with maintaining this item in inventory.

Step 5: Enter the data into a table such as the example below, or compute the EOQ by graphing the costs. This can also be accomplished by use of a mathematical formula. See the Appendix for the details.

Examples:

Example 1: Ordering an Item to Inventory

In the calculated table and chart, below, the following data are used:

Quantity used per year: 20,000; Carrying cost: $0.115 per item in inventory per year; Ordering Cost: $46.00 per order. To calculate the average carrying cost, we use one half of the quantity as a multiplier. The reason for this is because, for example, if we start with 20,000 units on January first and don't reorder until we've reached 0 at the end of the year, we only have an average of 10,000 units on hand.

Orders / yr	1	2	3	4	5	6	7	8
Quantity	20,000	10,000	6,667	5,000	4,000	3,333	2,857	2,500
Carrying Cost	$1150	$575	$383	$288	$230	$192	$164	$144
Ordering Cost	$46	$92	$138	$184	$230	$276	$322	$368
Total Cost	$1196	$667	$521	$472	$460	$468	$486	$512

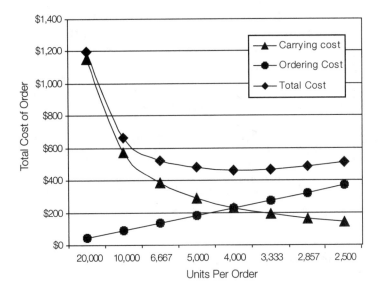

The preceding graph and the table both show 5 orders per year as generating the lowest cost per item. This means that if you order this item in lot sizes more or less than 4,000 units, you'll ultimately pay more per unit.

Example 2: Equipment Maintenance Scheduling

Rather than detail this second example with a table, the chart below simply shows the big picture to help the reader understand how the concept can be applied outside the inventory management

Maintenance costs include the repair person's time, supplies and minor parts, etc. Lost Production costs include the delays caused by downtime: lost customer orders, changed schedules for the workers resulting in pay for no work or else overtime, etc.

If the company performs no maintenance at all, the equipment will eventually break down resulting in unscheduled downtime and high costs, including parts that have broken and created further problems (think of never changing your car's oil until it runs out). On the other hand, if the company performs maintenance every day on the same equipment, they'll have excessive maintenance costs and reduced production. There has to be a balance. If you can quantify the costs, EOQ concepts can be applied to the problem.

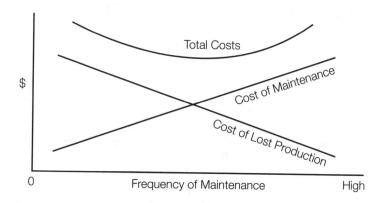

Tool #18: Break Even Analysis

Overview:

Break Even Analysis is a technique for determining whether or not it will be profitable to undertake a specific project. It can be applied to decisions dealing with manufacturing, inventory, purchasing, etc.

Knowledge or Input Required:

In order to use break even analysis, the decision maker must know: (1) The Fixed Costs associated with this product or organizational unit, (2) the Variable costs associated with the product or service, and (3) the anticipated volume of product or service produced and resulting income generated.

Results or Data Output Provided:

Application of this tool will help to decide whether or not it is feasible to produce a product, provide a service, maintain an inventory, etc. It gives a volume level below which it is not cost effective to do so.

Step by Step Instructions:

Step 1: Define the project or inventory item which you will analyze.
Step 2: Determine the fixed and variable costs associated with this project or item.

- **Fixed Costs** are costs which will be incurred regardless of the level of operation, and based simply on the fact that we are open for business. Changes in volume produced or serviced will not materially alter this cost. Examples are office rent, management salary, lighting, heating, minimum phone charge, etc.
- **Variable Costs** are those which vary in direct proportion to the volume of product or service or inventory. These include such costs as materials, supplies, direct labor, among others.
- **Semi-Variable or Step Variable Costs** are those which go up or down at predetermined points, such as when an additional shift is required, an additional supervisor is hired, when a quantity discount goes into effect, etc.

Step 3: Determine the income level to be generated by the product or service. This is usually price times units. It might vary if the price is discounted for volume or the market is saturated, therefore additional units can't be sold for the same price. This is possible, but it's practical to ignore this detail for most approximations.

Step 4: Create a table or plot a graph to display the data. The point at which the total revenue line crosses the total cost line is the "break even point." This means that service or product sales less than that volume will probably result in a loss, while sales above that level will result in a profit.

Example:

Your company is considering opening up an office in Toledo. If that is done, a fixed cost of operation of $6,000 per month is expected. That includes the cost of rent, office equipment, a receptionist and sending your Cleveland manager over one day a week to make sure the receptionist is not sleeping in the broom closet (even though she doesn't have any work to do yet). At a later point, we'll staff a full time manager.

The variable costs include hiring a salesperson & getting some order forms. The salesperson works on commission only. He, she or it gets $50 per unit sold, including all benefits. The gizmo being sold costs $100 to make. It sells for $249.

Number of Units Made	0	10	60	61	70	80
Fixed Cost	$6000	$6000	$6000	$6000	$6000	$6000
Variable Cost	$150	$150	$150	$150	$150	$150
Unit Price	$249	$249	$249	$249	$249	$249
Total Cost	$6000	$7500	$15000	$15150	$16500	$18000
Total Income	$0	$2490	$14940	$15189	$17430	$1920
Profit (Loss)	($6000)	($5010)	($60)	$39	$930	$1920

Question: how many gizmos must be sold per month in order to make it worthwhile to open the office in Toledo?

Answer: We begin to make a profit with the 61st. See the example table (on the previous page) and chart (below). There is, of course, also a mathematical means for calculating this (see the Appendix).

Similar analyses could be made to determine whether a grocery store should stock a new product which is offered, and many other kinds of questions.

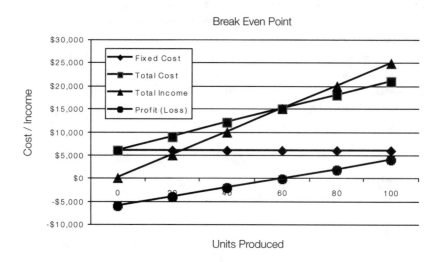

Break Even Point

Tool #19: Queuing Analysis

Overview:

Queuing analysis is sometimes called "waiting line theory." The word comes from the British use of "queue," or line. It is a means of analyzing the number and nature of servers necessary to handle a workload in a timely manner. Common examples of queuing problems include determining the number of clerks needed in a grocery store or the number of machines needed to prevent a bottleneck in a manufacturing process. A supervisor can easily do simple models of queuing by collecting data and doing a manual simulation. Queuing is actually subject to a number of sophisticated statistical techniques, so a complicated queuing analysis would require help of a computer model.

This is an effective technique, but may require collecting quite a bit of information. Random sampling (Chapter Five) and random number tables (see the appendix) may be helpful, depending on the nature of the problem you're analyzing. The mathematical formula for simple queuing analysis is explained in the Appendix. It's probably best to work through the examples below before turning to the appendix or studying the mathematics.

Most situations to which queuing can apply will have unpreventable periods of delay for customers and idleness for workers. While these should be minimized, it will normally be impossible to eliminate both since they are opposing or countervailing forces (see the earlier explanation on page 153). The relative costs of each should influence your decision as to which (immediate service or human resource efficiency) should be sacrificed.

Knowledge or Input Required:

In order to develop a queuing analysis, the manager or analyst needs to know: (1) How often and in what pattern customers (or products) arrive for service, (2) How long it takes to service a customer or product, and (3) The costs of customers kept waiting and of idle servers (employees or equipment).

Results or Data Output Provided:

The result of a queuing analysis is a projection of how many servers are needed at various workload levels. Since it frequently relies on sampling and variable data, it is seldom exactly correct. Nevertheless, it provides an appropriate basis for decision making. The accuracy of the estimate increases with a larger number of samples and with less variation among inputs such as service time or arrival frequency.

Step by Step Instructions:

Step 1: Define the process (operation) and inputs (customers or products requiring service) in order to insure a focus on the collection of data. Data can either be collected on a real time (historical) basis, or a simulation model can be created using a random number table and limited factual data collected from knowledgeable individuals or a short sampling of the operation.

- It is axiomatic that total capacity for service **must exceed** total demand. For example, if you have 500 customers per 8 hour day, and each one takes an average of 20 minutes to serve, you absolutely must have 21 servers. (500 ÷ 8 ÷ 3) It cannot be done with fewer. But to do it with ONLY 21, the 500 customers must come in at a perfectly smooth arrival rate (or else have to wait), and the 21 workers would each get less than half a minute rest all day. No vacations or breaks, either. Obviously, this is not likely unless your servers are machines. Even then, an allowance for maintenance time and system breakdowns should be included.

Step 2: Determine how often and in what pattern customers arrive for service in the system. This may be done by checking historical work records, by observing over a reasonable period of time, or by combining either of those with a simulation model based on random numbers. The data needs to be handled in one of the following ways:

A. If the arrival pattern is **relatively consistent** throughout the time period, you need only to determine an average time between arrivals.

B. If the arrival pattern is **variable, but predictable**, high and low periods will occur. In this case, you need to stratify the data (see Chapter Five) so you can determine server requirements by time or by day using an average arrival for each time period. For example, if Mondays are always the busiest, and other days are equal, set up two server patterns: one for Mondays and one for other days. If certain hours of the day are busier, determine average arrivals during each time period, e.g.: 8 to 10am, 10 to Noon, Noon to 2pm, or any other stratification which makes sense with the data.

C. If the arrival pattern is **variable in an apparently random fashion,** averages may give you weak data. The best option is to use a simulation model to determine optimum levels, and try to have flexible workers and work which can be moved to fill unexpectedly low demand times.

Step 3: Determine how long it takes to service a customer. Replace the words "arrival pattern" with "service time" in the explanation following step 2, above.

Step 4: Determine the costs associated with customers kept waiting and idle servers. Estimate the cost of customers waiting versus the cost of idle servers by collecting information on such things as these:

• **Customers:** Can they take their business elsewhere if the wait is too long? If the customers are parts waiting for service, can this be outsourced or subcontracted? What is the cost of a lost or dissatisfied customer? What do customers consider a reasonable time to wait? If the customer is a "product" in process, what does the delay add to the cost through increased work in process inventory? Will final shipments be delayed, or can time be made up elsewhere?

• **Servers:** Are employees paid by the hour or the job? Are other tasks available if the server is not busy? (For example, can cashiers also stock inventory, or is this prohibited by union or skill levels or logistics?) Can servers be sent home or called in to meet unexpected workload variations? Are there differences in skills required? **Note:** If there are, you may also need to stratify arrivals and service time data by type of skilled server required to do the job. If the "server" is a work station or piece of equipment, what is the real cost of installing additional units and of having idle capacity? *An important point:* Idle capacity may not be a realistic concern. Students are referred to studies on total quality manufacturing and books such as *The Goal* by Eliyahu Goldratt and Jeff Cox.

These costs are opposing forces, and — if graphed — would resemble the Economic Order Quantity model (see Tool # 17). At some point it will be cost effective to add another server, rather than requiring customers to wait longer.

Step 5: Collect data on arrivals and service, either by observation, keeping a log, or simulation of the data you now have using random numbers.

Step 6: Using the data collected in step 5 and the minimum servers as a starting point, determine the cost of adding one server at a time and the savings from reduced waiting time for the customer (this includes things listed under step 4). When costs go up more than savings, you have reached the optimum staffing or service provider level under the model.

Example:
Selling Theater Tickets

The following table (page 162) represents a simple queuing model. This is a movie theater on a busy street. It has one ticket window, and the movie is one of those you can go into and out of at any time. (This allows us to disregard the starting time for the moment. I've seen a few movies that could be watched starting and ending at any point in it, and it doesn't make any difference. Most of them either were made in Europe somewhere or starred Meryl Streep. Anyhow, just play along for now, OK? If it really is beyond your imagination, pretend you're going into the theater to see *Headline News*. It just keeps going and going and going and....)

Other necessary information is that customers arrive at regular intervals every 9 seconds. They look at the marquee and flip a coin to decide if they'll go in or not. If they get a head, they'll go in; if a tail, they'll not go in. If they do go in, it takes 12 seconds to buy a ticket. On the average, then, a customer wants to buy a ticket every 18 seconds and can be served in 12 seconds. Note that capacity exceeds demand, but there will still be waiting lines.

With plenty of total capacity for serving, we still find customers waiting 9 out of 15 times they choose to attend the show in our example.

If we had two servers, there would almost never have been a wait. Of course, the cost of service would approximately double. Question: Would increased patronage of the theater make up for that cost? We don't know.

Let's assume that five of the nine people who would have waited during those four minutes would have gone on without buying if there had been a line. Now, let's put some other assumptions around the problem. We'll say that staffing another position would cost $8 an hour (plus cost of another ticket machine which we'll say adds $2 an

Time	Toss	Begin Service	End Service	Wait?	Time Spent
000-008	T	—-	—-	-	0
009-017	H	9	20	N	12
018-026	T	—-	—-	-	0
027-035	H	27	38	N	12
036-044	T	—-	—-	-	0
045-053	T	—-	—-	-	0
054-062	H	54	65	N	12
063-071	H	66	77	Y	15
072-080	H	78	89	Y	18
081-089	H	90	101	Y	21
090-098	T	—-	—-	-	0
099-107	H	102	113	Y	15
108-116	H	114	125	Y	18
117-125	T	—-	—-	-	0
126-134	H	126	137	N	12
135-143	H	138	149	Y	15
144-152	T	—-	—-	-	0
153-161	T	—-	—-	-	0
162-170	H	162	173	N	12
171-179	H	174	185	Y	15
180-188	H	186	197	Y	18
189-197	T	—-	—-	-	0
198-207	T	—-	—-	-	0
208-215	T	—-	—-	-	0
216-224	T	—-	—-	-	0
225-233	H	225	236	N	12
234-242	H	237	248	Y	15

hour over its life). Each ticket sale brings a profit of $1.

If the four minutes represented by the table were stretched to an hour (multiply it by 15), we would have had approximately 75 people decide not to see the movie because of the line.

So we can see that an investment of $10 an hour in additional staffing and equipment will increase revenues by a $75. **This is true even though the current system has adequate capacity over the total day to easily handle the customers.** In fact, with two people there, each will be working only about 1/3 the time. Still, it's more profitable, according to the analysis, to pay them to be there!

Even with two servers, it's possible that a wait would happen. The odds of that are so low (less than 1%), that adding a third ticket window would never pay off, either in the short run or the long run.

"This taught me a lesson, but I'm not sure what it is."

– John McEnroe, on losing to Tim Mayotte in the U.S. Pro Indoor Championships

---

The computer support disk included with this book has a more extended example of queueing for those who are interested. The mathematical formula for a simple queuing analysis is described in the appendix.

Other Analysis Tools

Linear programming is a technique by which a manager or analyst can determine the best mix of products or services to maximize use of the organization's resources. The reader who has taken an economics course will remember the classic "guns or butter" examples where a country can either produce X number of guns or Y number of pounds of butter. By producing some of both, the country makes better uses of its resources. This is a useful tool, but is not covered in this text due to the mathematics involved. See an advanced management text or a statistics text for further information.

Transportation modeling is a special case of linear programming, and can be used by a manager or analyst to determine the best routing of materials or finished goods from multiple warehouses or producers to multiple plants or customers. It requires matrix algebra in the computation.

A variety of other tools and techniques can be found in project management, statistics, and advanced principles of management textbooks.

*A bonus tool called **Decision Tables** is described on the computer suppport disk which comes with this book.*

SUMMARY

This has been a detailed chapter with several more complex tools introduced. The most generic of all the tools in this chapter is the decision matrix which can be used to bring order to one's thinking about nearly any decision.

The expected value matrix is a special case of the decision matrix where the cells in the matrix can be completed with real numbers, rather than index numbers. The expected value concept was then applied to a decision tree which is a way to visualize more complex matrices.

Decomposition trees are another visual tool to help understand the make up of certain complex items (a budget, organizational staffing, etc.). They can be used with Pareto Analysis to help set priorities for action.

Scatter diagrams are yet another visual tool (though they can be quantified with correlation and regression analysis). These are used to indicate the relationship or lack of relationship between sets of data.

Economic order quantity analysis (EOQ) can really be used for more than inventory management, though it is normally used for that purpose. Break even analysis also can be used in a variety of decision making or problem solving situations.

Queuing analysis, though somewhat complex, is an excellent tool for scheduling and improving operations. Like many of the tools in this chapter, it can be handled with statistical formulae or computer programs.

Linear programming and some other tools were briefly mentioned, but not covered in detail.

Study Questions:

1. When should you use a weighted decision matrix?
2. How is an expected value matrix different from a weighted decision matrix?
3. Can you create a decision tree with more than three initial branches?
4. Is it ever possible to earn exactly the expected value projected from a decision tree?
5. What would you expect a scatter diagram to look like if you were to chart age (birth to death) against personal income?
6. Does it ever pay to intentionally have more people or equipment available for service than are minimally needed to serve the expected demand?

Exercises:

- Make a weighted decision matrix to help decide about an upcoming purchase.
- Create a decomposition tree for the job of being a student in a class.
- List the information the Dean of Business would need to collect to calculate a break even point for running a class on decision making.

CHAPTER

11

Tools to Determine Operational Productivity

"Never use the excuse of following orders as the rationale for following a poor course of action."

– Roger Meade

Chapter Objectives:

This chapter is designed to enable the reader to ....

- Understand when and how to use operations audits.
- Understand when and how to use work sampling.
- Understand when and how to use flow process charts.
- Be aware of several other productivity measuring techniques.

The tools in Chapter 11 relate to the concepts covered in Chapter 5.

The tools presented in this chapter are all techniques which a manager or supervisor can use to collect information about productivity of operations. Most come from an industrial engineering basis, but are presented here in a way which (hopefully) removes the mystique.

OPERATIONS AUDIT is a simple technique from the industrial engineer's bag of tricks. It requires only the abilities to ask questions, multiply and add. Any supervisor can use it to help determine data on such things as nature of work accomplished, amount of machine downtime, mixture of human and other resource skills needed, etc. It is frequently combined with other data collection and analysis tools.

WORK SAMPLING can be used to determine a number of things about a business operation: the productivity, the mix of employee skills needed, and much more.

FLOW PROCESS CHARTS also can be used by supervisors without quantitative training. They help to understand and structure operations in a way which lends itself to easy analysis.

A number of other tools will be briefly covered in the final section, but these three are the only ones to be discussed in detail.

As mentioned with all the previous tools in this book, these techniques will not give any absolute answers. They *will* provide information to *help* in decision making, but the final decision usually involves a certain amount of risk.

Tool #20: Operations Audit

Overview:

Operations audit is a process to collect information on a work operation of nearly any kind. Among industrial engineering techniques, this one has a relatively low level of sophistication. It is, however, very flexible and user friendly.

If the auditor or supervisor doing the audit is familiar with the work, it will be easier. This process is intrusive to the operation, meaning that it takes employee time away from production, so the auditor should attempt to do as much as possible in preparing. Work sampling (Tool #21) is a less intrusive means of getting the information, but takes more skill on the analyst's part and takes longer to collect the data. Data from operations audit is more specific than that collected from work sampling.

Knowledge or Input Required:

Workers must be interviewed and production records verified by the person doing the audit. This requires some interpersonal and research skills. A good starting point is to create a decomposition tree (see Chapter Ten) for the work unit being studied.

Results or Data Output Provided:

Using operations audit, a manager or analyst can determine the kinds of tasks performed by individual workers and the amount of time expended on these. The data from an OA can then be used to do a work distribution analysis. The result of the OA is input to decision making on how to rearrange tasks to improve workflow or efficiency, determination of equipment or staffing needs and other aspects of operations management.

Step by Step Instructions:

Step 1: Define the work center to be studied. Data is usually collected on a group of employees who do similar work and/or work on the production of the same product or service. The group can be as small as one person, but it's more practical and informative to use larger groups.

Step 2: The analyst or person responsible for collecting the data should work with the employees to draw up a list of all major tasks accomplished in the work center. Make this list in one column on the left side of sheets of paper. A major task, in this sense, should be something which produces some output (a sale, a widget, a letter, etc.) and is countable. It should not be so small as "enters number into computer," rather a much larger grouping of events. A typical work center might have 20 to 80 major tasks. Even if only some employees in the work center are responsible for the task, it should be included.

Step 3: For each task listed, determine the number of times it is completed per month. (If you find it more practical, you could use weeks or days or years. Simply make sure all data is collected on or converted to the same basis.) List this information in a second column. The more accurate your counts, the better the data. It may be helpful to validate the frequency of task performance by checking historical records, keeping a log for a week or two, etc.

Step 4: For each task listed, determine the amount of time it takes to perform that task once. If there's variation, attempt to determine an average. Again, the better the data, the more accurate the final result. Verify times by observation or historical record when possible. Verification is more important with high frequency of occurrence tasks or those which take fairly long to perform each time. Put this in a third column beside each task.

Step 5: Multiply the time and frequency associated with each task to come up with a total task time, and enter that in a fourth column. Add amounts in the fourth column to determine total workcenter time over the month.

Step 6: Do a reality check. Your author remembers the first time he was involved in this sort of a study, over 30 years ago. The first effort was with the workload of an executive secretary in the organization, a grandmotherly type named Mrs. Seitsinger. When the computations were done, it seemed she was working 327 hours a month. The organizational standard was 142 hours per month per employee authorization. I revisited her, we had a good laugh about her being triplets, then recalculated some of the times and frequencies to make them more accurate and realistic.

Example:

Below is an operations audit of a mailroom operation. The data was collected by interviewing the mailroom operator.

Operations Audit of Mail Room

Task/Activity	Time	Count	Monthly Total
1. Pick up/Delivery of Mail	40 min	2/day	28.9 hrs
2. Courier to Post Office	60 min	2/day	43.4 hrs
3. Sorting internal mail for distribution	25 min	2/day	18.1 hrs
4. Labeling and metering outgoing	35 min	40/mo	23.3 hrs
5. Weekly Staff Meeting	50 min	1/wk	3.6 hrs
6. Newsletter preparation	6 hours	1/mo	6.0 hrs
7. Ordering supplies, stamps	40 min	3/mo	2.0 hrs
8. Packaging outgoing materials	10 min	80/mo	13.3 hrs
9. Customer service at counter	4 min	15/day	21.7 hrs
Total Work Required			160.3 hr/mo
Total employees required			1.08+

Notes: Computation based on industry standard of 8.0 hours = 1 day; 21.7 days = 1 month; 4.35 weeks = 1 month. An hourly employee is expected to work 148 hours per month which allows for vacation, daily breaks, holidays and sick time allowance.

High time/frequency items should be verified. For example, if the trips to the Post Office actually take only 55 minutes, there's a difference of 3.50 hours per month in the total. This mailroom operation would require one person to work some overtime, or two people to work part time.

Tool #21: Work Sampling

Overview:

Work Sampling is a means of gathering information about a workplace. As the name implies, it is a sampling of the work done over time. While this is an industrial engineering technique, virtually any manager or supervisor can apply it to his or her own work setting. This is accomplished by taking "samples" of the work being done in a workplace.

Knowledge or Input Required:

The person doing the data collection must be available for several days to make observations of the work center activity. This data collection technique applies only to observable work done in a reasonably concentrated work area. It would not be possible, for example, to use this tool to gather data about a field sales force or maintenance department which goes to other work areas to complete their jobs.

It is appropriate to consider what else goes on in the work center over the period of a year. If the workload is especially heavy or light at the time the sample is taken, adjustments to the data may be appropriate. Likewise, if several people are out sick or other unusual things are going on, the decision makers should consider how the data is influenced by those facts.

Results or Data Output:

Results can be used to determine staffing requirements, equipment needs, types of skill needed in various ratios, and – of course -- budget requirements can be determined based on the other information developed.

Step by Step Instructions:

Step 1: Determine the work group to be measured. Usually a group is defined as all persons working in one location who do similar work and/or work on the production of the same product or service. The group can be as small as one person, but it's more practical and informative to use larger groups. Although the work setting will influence exact numbers, each person responsible for collecting data may be able to handle observing up to thirty or so employees during the study.

Step 2: Group the work accomplished by these employees into a collection of easily identifiable task categories. One category needs to be "idle." Fewer than four categories or more than a dozen become impractical. To determine the categories, talk with the supervisor and employees who do the job. See the example following these steps.

Step 3: Arrange a data collection schedule. The person(s) responsible for collecting the data need to understand what each category looks like as it's being done and know which employees are part of the study. A data collection sheet must be constructed listing people, task categories (using numbers is easier than writing things out), and times at which the samples will be taken. The times can be as simple as "on the quarter hours" or done on a basis of random numbers (see the Appendix) to get a mixed observation schedule. If the employees can not control when work is done (e.g., an assembly line or customer service counter), structured samples are fine. Random samples are better when work is controllable. This prevents workers from delaying work until the sample time.

Step 4: Gather the data by observing and recording what tasks employees are performing at the scheduled sample times. The larger the total number of samples, the greater the accuracy will be. See the table in Appendix A for the number of samples needed to obtain 98% confidence of being within 3% accuracy. The sampling period should extend over at least a week or a complete cycle of work, if the work is cyclical on a monthly basis or less. Often the data collected the first few days is higher than it should be, since the employees are conscious of being watched. Occasionally, then, employees are less productive the third or fourth days as they run out of things. It may be appropriate to consider the data from the first three or four days to be a "trial run," and not use it.

Step 5: When sufficient data has been collected, compute the percentage of total work done in each category. This stratified information can then be used to determine what skills are needed, what type or amount of equipment is needed, and many other pieces of information.

Examples:

Example #1: Office Administration Work Group

The table below represents a study of a clerical pool for a large corporation. Twenty workers are observed on a random basis twice per hour over ten days to get the data. Note that the categories are observable, limited (only 6), and tied to certain levels of skill (e.g., taking and transcribing dictation is different pay rate than keyboarding). After ten days of data collection, samples in each of the categories came out like this:

Category of Work	Samples	Percentage
Keyboarding / Data Entry	940	26%
Filing / Obtaining Files	420	12%
Taking / Transcribing Dictation	200	6%
Telephone Communication	680	19%
Researching Internet / Databases	860	24%
Idle & Lunch Break	500	13%
Totals	3,600	100%

Notes: There are currently 20 persons employed in this work center. Using the above data, what can you project about the needs of the workplace? (Statistically, 3600 samples brings the accuracy confidence to within 2% on each category.) If keyboarding/data entry is a specific job classification in this company, how many of these persons are needed out of the 20? (Answer: at least six.) If dictation is a separate and more highly paid category, how many of these persons are needed? (at least two) How many transcription machines? (at least two) If everyone were 100% productive, how many employees are really needed in this work center? (18, but that's not good planning unless they can work overtime.)

Don't make the mistake of trying to match things too tightly. For example, it is logistically impossible and managerially impractical to operate the sample work center with 17.4 employees. People need to go to lunch, to take breaks, and to have some time to move among tasks. Further, people will be absent or on vacation at times. Actually, 20 people will keep quite busy, especially since lunch is included in the measurement. (It could have been separated & left out of the calculation.)

Further, having only two transcription machines and only two persons qualified for dictation is not a good idea. (1) These people will be absent, on vacation, at lunch, or otherwise unavailable at times. One person would not be able to do the job without extensive overtime. (2) Because requests for dictation probably don't come in on a completely smooth basis, there will be times when the workload peaks and requests come in groups. You could study this potential problem using queuing analysis (Tool #19).

Example #2: Work Sampling in the Shipping–Receiving Unit

Category of Work	Observations	Percentage
Loading & Unloading Trucks (Manual)	420	16.6
Loading & Unloading Trucks (Forklift)	540	21.3
Crating / Wrapping Goods for Shipment	605	23.9
Inventory including bar code scans	185	7.3
Documentation & Secretarial Duties	225	8.9
Order planning & tracing	120	4.7
Supervision, Training	160	6.3
Other, special tasks (code & note)	80	3.2
Idle, in work center	195	7.7
Totals	2,530	100

Notes: 19 persons were sampled for 9 days at 2 observations per hour, which generated 2916 samples. There were also 386 "n/a" samples which included breaks, vacation, out sick or other excused absence from area. This allows "idle" samples to be distinguished from legitimate reasons for not working. Therefore, the data excludes information on workers not present, so the "idle" actually reflects the percentage of time people should have been working, assuming work was available.

If "forklift driver" is a separate category, how many of these do we need in this cost center? At least 4 (16.6% x 19 workers = 3.15). If the workload and excused absences during the study was typical, how many people are really needed? 17.54 (92.3% x 19). Since all excused time was already eliminated from the computation, it's pretty certain that at least one person could be eliminated from this operation without requiring overtime -- as long as the workload is relatively stable. Other such decisions can be made on the basis of the data represented above.

Tool #22: Flow Process Charts

Overview:

Flow Process Charts are industrial engineering tools to help a manager observe, record and analyze an operation. They can be used to follow either a physical product or an office or service operation. Also, the observer can chart either the product (material) as it progresses through assembly or treatment, or the individual doing the work.

A form of some kind (see the sample which follows) is used to organize, record and analyze data.

Many data collection or depiction formats exist for similar purposes. The whole idea of work flow charting is, of course, applied to computer programs (using different symbols) to help the designers and users understand the software operation and requirements. Some of the recent research on services design uses different symbols.

Knowledge or Input Required:

To create a flow process chart, the analyst must understand the steps in the process being evaluated or charted, and measure times needed and distance covered in completing each of the steps. A form is useful for this process.

Results or Data Output Provided:

The flow process chart gives you a structured tool for analysis of the process being evaluated. It organizes data in a useful fashion to suggest questions that the analyst might ask. A revised flow process chart serves as a training tool, and allows before and after comparisons of the operation.

Step by Step Instructions:

Step 1: Define the operation which will be charted. It is best to deal with a complete cycle of production or complete part of the operation performed by one individual.

Step 2: (OPTIONAL) If appropriate, draw a scaled layout of the workplace to determine physical flow of the product, paperwork or individual being charted.

Step 3: Complete the headings on a blank flow process chart (see example format).

Step 4: Observe the operation, writing down each task in order. Verify with the operator (or supervisor) that the chart correctly describes all the tasks in the order needed to complete the operation.

Step 5: Estimate, check documentation, or observe and measure the operation to determine the time necessary to complete each task. Record this on the chart. ALSO, measure and record distances moved for any aspect of the operation.

Step 6: Determine which of the five categories applies to each stage (task) of the operation. Indicate this on the chart by marking the appropriate symbol. The standard symbols are:

Flow Process Chart Symbols

○ **Operations** – the individual works or something is physically done to the product. These activities are indicated by a circle.

→ **Transportations** – the individual goes from one place to another or the product is moved from one place to another. This is indicated by an arrow and distance indication.

■ **Inspection** – the individual inspects work or the product for completeness or accuracy. These activities are indicated by a square.

❙ **Delay** – the individual has to wait for something to happen or the product must await the next activity to be performed. This is indicated by a capital D or semi-circle.

▼ **Storage** – the product is put into inventory (finished goods or work-in-process) until the next activity to be performed is about to happen. This is indicated by a triangle. It does not apply to individuals when the worker (rather than material) is being charted.

Step 7: Total the times, distances, and number of tasks in each category, and record these totals in the area provided on the chart.

Step 8: Working with employees, supervisors, or any other individuals who would be affected by a change, systematically question each part of the operation. Appropriate questions would include:

- Is the operation necessary?
- Can it be combined, automated, done elsewhere (in house or contract)?
- Can it be modified to simplify or improve the workflow?
- Can any transportations be eliminated, reduced in distance or made less often?
- Are inspections done before critical points at which costs are involved?
- Can inspections be combined or done less often or done only on a sample of the output?
- Can delays be reduced or eliminated?
- Is storage only at beginning or end of the operation? If not, can it be changed?
- Examine the layout (if drawn) for evidence of repeated backtracking or poor location of workers or poor flow of product or workers.

Step 9: Prepare a new proposed/trial flow process chart (and/or layout) as answers to the questions in step 8 suggest improvements. Again, work with the operators to confirm the design and test the changes.

Example:

The example below shows the flow process chart for an "Authorization to Investigate" form in the Claims Department of an Insurance company.

No.	Details of Method Present ☐ Proposed ☐	Operation	Transportation	Inspection	Delay	Storage	Distance (ft.)	Quantity	Time in Min
	Flow Process Chart of Form 3355 Preparation								
1	Remove Claim Dept's request from in-basket and identify client.	○							0.2
2	Walk to filing area, locate file, and return to desk.	○	→				55		3.2
3	Locate pertinent information in client file.	○							0.5
4	Enter information on "Authorization to Investigate" Form (#3355)	○							4.7
5	Inspect form for accuracy.			■					0.5
6	Walk to section leader's desk.		→				35		1.0
7	Wait for signature.				▶				2.0
8	Walk back to desk		→				35		1.0
9	Tear form apart into separate sheets.	○							0.2
10	Prepare regional investigator's copy for mailing.	○							1.8
11	Prepare Claim Dept's copy for routing; place in mail basket on desk.	○							1.5
12	Place one copy in client's file.	○							0.2
13	Walk to filing area, re-file, & return to desk.	○	→			▼	55		2.4
	Total Counts	9	4	1	1	1	180	N/A	20.2

The purpose is to force a step-by-step analysis of the process. This establishes a starting point to study ways to reduce distance, movement, idle time and unneeded operations or inspections in the process.

Other Productivity Measurement Tools

Productivity measuring tools come in many other forms. **Motion time study**, for example, was originated and developed in the late 1800's through early 1900's by famous names in management history including Frederick Winslow Taylor and the husband and wife team of Frank and Lillian Gilbreth (of "Cheaper By the Dozen" fame). It has relatively narrow use and requires quite a bit of training and practice to do well, so it's not included in this tool collection. If you or your team might consider bringing in someone to perform a motion time study, the job needs to be highly standardized, highly repetitive (hundreds per week), visible work (management tasks can't be motion time studied, for example), and no more than partially limited by machine time.

Work distribution charting is a technique sometimes used with work sampling or operations audit (Tools 20 & 21) to tie the tasks recorded in those activities to one individual or job classification in order to analyze the operation in more detail. With the increased emphasis on teamwork and interchangeability or flexibility of job assignments, this technique is being used less, but it still has its purpose.

New techniques in productivity analysis have emerged with the computer. For example, companies can now buy software to put resident in PC's (or on a network) which will record and report on time and effectiveness of use by the PC operators. Likewise, many telemarketing operations use automated equipment to track employees' time on phone calls. In fact, workplace surveillance is an issue in union contracts and lawsuits regarding employer ethics.

Many of the previously discussed tools and techniques such as control charts, sampling, probability, etc., also have applicability in productivity measurement. Since quality and production control are often concerned with productivity issues, many TQM programs, JIT programs, etc., make wide use of productivity analyzing tools.

Summary

This chapter has presented how-to-do it instructions for three simple industrial engineering techniques: operations audit, work sampling, and flow process charting.

Study Questions:

1. When would you use each of the three techniques described in this chapter?
2. What are some of the problems associated with operations audit?
3. What are some of the problems associated with work sampling?

Exercise:

• Talk with an industrial engineer about the different techniques described in this chapter. Which does she or he use? What others are used and for what purposes?

APPENDICES

A. Formulas and
   Mathematical
   Notes for Tools

B. References &
   Bibliography

C. Contents and Use
   of the Computer
   Support Disk

A s explained in the Foreword, the purpose of this text is to be as user-friendly as possible and to avoid mathematical complications. Bill Waterson (in the persona of Calvin of the sorely-missed Calvin and Hobbes comic strip) once referred to mathematics as a "...religion, therefore something which should not be taught in schools."

Nonetheless, much of what has been included in this book does have a mathematical basis. So for those of you who enjoy things composed of Greek letters, subscripts, set notation, and the like, here's some fun reading for you. Enjoy! The rest of you may ignore this. You're welcome.

Chapter 5 – Gathering & Analyzing Information

Normal curve

The so-called Normal (or Bell-shaped) Curve is a standard concept in statistics. It is often used in control processes because it can be used to measure deviation from the standard or norm. If you refer to the discussion of rolling dice in Chapter Five (page 59), the frequency with which each possible number occurs approximates a normal bell curve. At the center is the most commonly occurring number (the "norm") of ways to come up with the number 7, and on each side, indicating less frequent occurrences, are the other numbers. See the figure below. A true normal curve is based on the binomial theorem (think coin flipping), and is actually a bit flatter with longer tails on each side. Its use allows such concepts as "standard deviation" and other measures of central tendency in data. You can use it to predict the likelihood of a data point being more than a certain distance from the average. For more information, take a course in statistics or consult a basic textbook in that field. Some are listed in the bibliography.

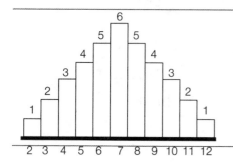

Probability of rolling each number with an honest pair of dice.

Combinations

Combinations are simple events in which the order of selection is not important. For example, eight horses are running a race and none of them tie. Calculate the number of combinations of horses possible for the first three finishers in any order.

The equation to compute this is: $\{n|r\} = \dfrac{n!}{(r!(n-r)!)}$

Where $\{n|r\}$ is the number of combinations of n objects taken r at a time. The notation "!" is called "factorial," and represents that integer multiplied by each integer less than itself. Therefore, 4! = 4 x 3 x 2 x 1 = 24.

So, for the above problem,

$$\{8|3\} = \frac{8!}{(3!)(8!-3!)} = \frac{8 \times 7 \times 6 \times 5 \times 4 \times 3 \times 2 \times 1}{(3 \times 2 \times 1)(5 \times 4 \times 3 \times 2 \times 1)} = 56$$

As another example, let's say a lottery is based on choosing 6 numbers out of 47. How many possible combinations of 6 out of 47 numbers exist? (It doesn't matter in which order they're drawn.)

$$\{47|6\} = \frac{47!}{6! \times 41!} = 10{,}737{,}573$$

So your odds of winning are 1 out of 10,737,573.

Permutations

Permutations are simple events in which the order of selection *is* important. With the above horse race example, how many possible permutations are there for eight horses to finish in 1st, 2nd and 3rd places? The equation for this is:

$\{n||r\} = n! / (n-r)!$

$$\{8|3\} = \frac{8!}{5!} = \frac{8 \times 7 \times 6 \times 5 \times 4 \times 3 \times 2 \times 1}{5 \times 4 \times 3 \times 2 \times 1} = 336$$

Question: You have six dinner guests to seat at a table (one at a time). How many possible ways can you do this? Answer: 6! / 1! = 6x5x4x3x2x1 /1 = 720. Amazing! Try it, if you wish. It will provide the night's entertainment and plenty of exercise!

Value of additional information

Several possible ways exist to evaluate the value of additional information. Let's begin by pointing out that the higher the relative probability (or expected value) of the best choice among alternatives, the less likely additional information will be valuable. Thus, if you have a 90% chance of earning $100, your expected value is $90. How much would you pay to insure that?

One way of thinking would say no more than $10, the difference between your expected value and the possible earnings. Another would say that you could spend $99 to insure you earned the $100, and still be $1 ahead of where you might have been (10% chance). So this issue, like many other things, depends on the framing (see Chapter Six).

Likewise, the value of *perfect information* is different than the value of *improved information*. With the former, you eliminate probabilities, and with the latter you simply change the probabilities for the better (but they're still not perfect).

As the text suggests, perhaps the best way to deal with this issue is to list the information you *could* get and how much it costs, then prioritize this information by how much it improves the odds of a correct decision. If, intuitively, the information is improved enough to justify the cost, then do it.

In statistics, you can look up Bayes' rule as a formal mathematical statement of the reasoning that supports the "expected opportunity loss" theory, but the subject is more complicated than can be covered here.

Sampling theory

Sampling theory is the subject of entire textbooks (albeit boring ones). The only concern we have for purposes of this book is to explain how many samples are needed to reach a given level of accuracy. In general, the more samples (properly taken samples, at least), the greater the accuracy. The level of accuracy is expressed in terms of plus or minus a certain percent accuracy at a specific level of confidence. For example, we might be 98% confident that our sample is ±3% accurate.

The first number is a probability (98% of the time under these conditions), while the other is a statement of relativity (the figures we have developed from our sample are within 3% of the actual population). The two terms work in tandem. Probability will increase (get higher) as the variation from population increases. For certain samples, it might be equally true to say that we are 95% confident of plus or minus 3% accuracy, or that we are 99% confident of plus or minus 10% accuracy.

You must start with the confidence level you wish to have. 90, 95, 98, and 99% are common choices in statistics. Given that, you determine the accuracy level based on the number of samples and the ratio of the samples in the largest category to the total samples. The following table indicates the samples needed for 3% accuracy at 98% confidence.

If the largest category in the sample is:					
5% or 95%	10% or 90%	20% or 80%	25% or 75%	40% or 60%	50%
You need this many samples to be 98% certain of estimations ±3% accurate.					
211	400	711	833	1067	1111

The computation of 400 samples for the table above is done using the following formula:

$$S = \frac{2\sqrt{P(1-P)}}{\sqrt{n}} \qquad\qquad .03 = \frac{2\sqrt{.9(.1)}}{\sqrt{400}}$$

$$N' = \frac{4(P - P^2)}{S^2} \qquad\qquad 400 = \frac{4(.9 - .9^2)}{.03^2}$$

Where S is the absolute accuracy (± .03, in this case)

P is the largest percentage occurrence for a single category

n is the total number of samples

N' is the number of samples needed to reach that accuracy at 98% confidence.

Probability

The concept of probability has to do with the "odds" of something happening. Sometimes you calculate these odds intuitively, such as the odds of pulling an ace out of an honest deck of cards (without jokers). You know there are four aces and fifty two cards, so the odds are 4 out of 52, 4/52, 0.07692, 1 in 13, or 12:1 (all different ways of saying the same thing). If you continue this and chart the results, it will look very much like the normal curve, discussed above.

Some of the basic facts about probability that might be useful include how to treat multiple probabilities. For example, we know the likelihood of getting a "head" on the flip of a fair coin is 50%. What is the likelihood of getting two heads in a row? or three heads in a row? Let's look at the possible options:

Two coins: TT, TH, HT, HH. Therefore, the likelihood of two heads is ¼th.

Three coins: TTT, TTH, THT, THH, HTT, HTH, HHT, HHH. Therefore, the likelihood of three heads is 1/8th.

If you have a probability of ½ on any single event, then the likelihood of that same result happening in multiple attempts is ½ multiplied by itself that number of times, or $(½)^n$, so if $n = 3$, the likelihood of three heads in a row is $(½)^3$ or $(½)(½)(½) = ⅛$.

What if the probability changes according to the result of the first event? Suppose you draw cards from an honest deck, and don't replace them? What would be the chance of drawing four aces in four draws? The chance of drawing one ace is 4/52. If you are successful and don't replace it, the chance of drawing a second one is 3/51, then 2/50, and 1/49. Just like above, you multiply to get the final probability, which in this case would be:

$$\frac{4}{52} \times \frac{3}{51} \times \frac{2}{50} \times \frac{1}{49} = \frac{24}{6,497,400} = \frac{1}{270,725} = 0.000003693$$

What if you want to know the probability of drawing an ace *or* a king? Logically, you would know that the probability for each is 4/52, and the combination would be 8/52. You can simply **add** probabilities when you are dealing with an "or" in the equation, as long as aces and kings are mutually exclusive.

Here's another. What is the probability of drawing an ace or a red card? These are not mutually exclusive. An ace may or may not be a red card, and vice versa. Calculate the answer as above, but subtract out the overlap. It would work out to the following equation.

$$\frac{4}{52} + \frac{26}{52} - \frac{2}{52} = \frac{28}{52}$$

Many other calculations can be made with probabilities, however those are beyond the scope of this textbook. Take a course in elementary business statistics or talk with your local bookie or numbers runner. They can enlighten you on the finer points of this subject.

Regression and Correlation

Suffice it to say that if you don't have a good reason to know this, you probably don't want to. Almost no one calculates this by hand anymore, because it's not fun, and because business calculators which sell for under $40 will do it (at least for a straight line) very easily. Curved lines are more complex. Doing calculations for this by hand has probably caused some people to go into *clinical* regression, but that's another story....

There are two things you might want to know about this stuff:

(1) The correlation coefficient. Essentially, this tells you how good the fit of a line is through the points. This is stated in terms of *r*, the coefficient of correlation. It ranges from -1 to +1. The closer the number is to either -1 or +1, the better the fit. 0.00 means there is no correlation at all, while 1.00 means the line goes through every point perfectly. (The sign has to do with the relationship of the numbers on the axes. If Y goes up when X goes down, a perfect correlation would be -1. If Y goes up when X goes up, a perfect correlation would be +1.)

(2) The regression equation. You might also want to know the mathematical equation for that line. This is called the regression equation. It allows you to express the relationship between the two factors on the axes in mathematical terms. This can be useful because, if you know one value (either the X or Y), you can calculate the other value according to the average.

If you really want the formulae to create the coefficient and equation from a set of data, check out a statistical reference book.

Chapter 10 – Tools to Compare and Evaluate Options

Decision Tree

Mathematical calculations of the decision tree probabilities are aimed at finding the branch of the tree with the highest probability or highest utility. It can be viewed in two basic ways:

(a) In one, the decision maker has to make an initial choice, choosing that path with the highest expected utility. Then, at every succeeding stage where a decision has to be made (having observed the consequences of his previous decision), choosing to move along the branch which offers him the highest utility.

Or:

(b) In the other view, the decision maker designs a series of strategies *before* he makes the first decision, then simply follows that strategy which gives him the highest utility.

The first is like making chess moves one at a time and waiting for your opponent's reaction. The second is a higher level of playing -- taking charge, so to speak. It requires more *a priori* knowledge, but may yield better results -- or it may not.

Again, Bayesian analysis would be useful, but such is beyond the scope of this text. Even the formula probably wouldn't be of much use except to impress your friends.

Economic Order Quantity

EOQ in its simplest form (no step variables, etc.) can be computed as:

$$EOQ = \sqrt{\frac{2OD}{HT}}$$

Where   **EOQ** = the economic order quantity expressed in units;
H = holding cost per unit;
D = Demand;
O = Order set-up cost;
and   **T** = Time period.

So for the example in the text (Tool #17), H = \$0.115; D = 20,000; O = \$46; T = 1

$$EOQ = \sqrt{\frac{2 \times 46 \times 20,000}{0.115 \times 1}} = 4,000 \text{ units}$$

Break-Even Point

In its simplest form (no step variables, etc.) the break even point can be computed as:

$$BEP = \frac{(FC)}{(SP - VC)}$$

Where   **BEP** is Break Even Point expressed in number of units
FC is the fixed cost associated with the project
SP is the selling price per unit
VC is the variable cost per unit produced

So, for the example in the text (Tool #18),

$$BEP = \frac{6000}{249 - 150} = 60.61 \text{ units}$$

More complex forms which include step variables will naturally require a more complex algorithm. Step variables, in this context, are situations where a fixed or variable cost changes at some point, for example if a quantity discount is available, such as a situation where the first 100 units cost \$9.00 each, but 101-1000 units will only cost \$8.00 each. Etc. An algorithm is a mathematical formula; it is not the dance moves of a former vice-president (you may remember, he is famous for having no rhythm).

Queuing Analysis

As you can tell from the discussion of queuing in the text (Tool #19), it can be a quite complicated process. If you have several variables or time stratifications, you will need a computer (or an awful lot of patience) to deal with the details. However, for the basic, no frills model of queuing analysis, you can use the following formula:

$$Pn = (1 - \frac{AR}{SR}) \times (\frac{AR}{SR})^n$$

Where   **Pn** is the probability of more than "n" customers waiting for service
AR is the average arrival rate
SR is the average service rate
n (as an exponent) is the number of customers.

So, let's say we don't want more than three customers to be waiting. Say customers arrive at an *average* of two per minute, and it takes an *average* of four minutes to serve a customer. Your basic staffing should be eight for this situation (2 per minute at 4 minutes each = 8). What is the probability of a customer having to wait?

$$P_3 = \left(1 - \frac{2}{4}\right) \times \left(\frac{2}{4}\right) = \frac{1}{2} \times \frac{1}{8} = \frac{1}{16}$$

This means there's a probability at any given time of more than three people having to wait of 1 in 16. As a management decision, if you're willing to put up with 4 or more customers in line 6.25% of the time (1 in 16), then eight people is enough to staff the service. If not, you must increase staffing accordingly. (Frankly, you would need some overtime if you have only eight, since the assumptions require are that they'd be busy 100% of the time.)

Chapter 11 – Tools to Determine Operational Productivity

Random Number Tables

Random number tables are a tool to help create a simulation of reality, among many other uses. They are normally used in situations where sampling and modeling are involved. We may want to simulate a business operation rather than take the time necessary to allow observation of that situation in the real world. Simulations could also be created so we can gather large amounts of data about the operation, or so we can try the operation in a variety of ways with different things going on.

For example, let's say we want to determine the likelihood of a telephone going unanswered in the office which was studied in the discussion of work sampling (Tool #21). We would need to combine this information with a queuing model (Tool #19), and simulate the occurrence of telephone calls. From the work sampling, we know that the total work in the office was 20 people doing the following tasks:

Keyboarding/Data Entry	26%	Filing/Obtaining Files	12%
Taking or Transcribing Dictation	06%	Telephone Communication	19%
Researching Internet/Databases	24%	Idle/Lunch	13%

We want to create a simulation in which these six activities will occur at the same rate of frequency as we found them in the workplace. To do this, we can watch the workplace for many days and see how often the phone is unanswered, or we can simulate many days' worth of observation by using a random number table.

A random number table is a list of numbers which appear in random order and have an equal likelihood of occurring. Random number tables can be found in the appendix of any statistical textbook, but you can use other sources, as well. For example, you could use a telephone directory and go down the number column using just the last 1, 2, 3 or 4 digits of the phone numbers. (Question: Why not the first 1, 2 or 3 digits? Answer: Most won't have 0's or 1's in the first two spots, and there will only be a few combinations in any single directory. Therefore, they are not random.) Some computer programs and calculators have random number generators, or you can pull cards out of a hat.

Here's a two-digit random number table you might find in a statistics textbook.

```
29  44  40  46  93  14  84  57  92  66  36  11  24  00  33  60  66  39  30  54
69  14  64  96  59  55  92  48  43  26  33  16  08  63  05  31  50  72  85  45
05  89  84  72  07  32  59  69  03  06  36  92  49  87  54  08  16  97  20  39
96  31  72  41  05  12  57  02  74  22  05  13  31  95  37  49  28  77  65  53
07  99  56  72  57  45  44  28  70  30  00  69  94  05  59  93  08  60  79  84
```

Most tables would take up an entire page, but this is adequate for our illustration.

To convert the work sampling data (above) to something we can use with a random number table, we have to set each category equal to certain digits. A simple way to do this would be:

Keyboarding/Data Entry	01-26	Filing/Obtaining Files	27-38
Taking or Transcribing Dictation	39-44	Telephone Communication	45-63
Researching Internet/Databases	64-87	Idle/Lunch	88-00

Then we read through the table in a consistent fashion (such as Left to Right and Top to Bottom), and indicate which activity our sample represents. Doing this with the above table, the first number is 29, so our first simulated activity is Filing. The second number is 44, so the second simulated activity is Dictation. Next is 40, also Dictation, followed by 46, Telephone, Etc.

Instead of watching the work center to get "real" information, which would take a long time, we can create a model (simulation) of the workplace quite quickly.

References and Bibliography

References Cited in this book:

Adams, James L., *Conceptual Blockbusting: A Guide to Better Ideas*, W.W. Norton (New York, 1974 and subsequent revised editions).

Beach, Lee R., *Making the Right Decision: Organizational Culture, Vision and Planning*, Prentice-Hall (Englewood Cliffs, NJ, 1993).

Bryson, Bill, *A Short History of Nearly Everything*, Broadway Books (New York, 2003).

Evans, James R., *Creative Thinking in the Decision and Management Sciences*, South Western (Cincinnati, 1991).

Goldratt, Eliyahu M. and Jeff Cox, *The Goal: A Process of Ongoing Improvement*, Revised Edition, North River Press (Croton-on-Hudson, NY, 1986).

Hisker, William J., *Critical Thinking Guide*, McGraw-Hill (New York, 1993)

Kahneman, Daniel and Amos Tversky, "Prospect Theory: An Analysis of Decision Under Risk." *Econometrica,* 47 (March 1979) pp. 263-291.

Kepner, Charles H., and Benjamin B. Tregoe, *The Rational Manager: A Systematic Approach to Problem Solving and Decision Making*, Kepner-Tregoe, Inc. (Princeton, NJ, 1965).

-----, *The New Rational Manager*, Princeton Research Press (Princeton, NJ, 1981).

McCall, Morgan M. Jr., and Robert F. Kaplan, *Whatever It Takes: The Realities of Managerial Decision Making*, Second Edition, Prentice Hall (Englewood Cliffs, NJ, 1990).

Nutt, Paul C., *Why Decisions Fail – Avoiding the Blunders and Traps that Lead to Debacles*, Berrett-Koehler Publishers (San Francisco, 2002)

Schwartz, Barry, *The Paradox of Choice: Why More Is Less*, Harper Perennial (New York, 2004).

Vaughn, Robert H., "Decision Making for Managers." *Trainer's Workshop* American Management Associations. Vol 7, No. 4 (July-August, 1993) pp. 3-64.

Vaughn, Robert H., *The Professional Trainer: A Comprehensive Guide to Planning, Delivering and Evaluating Training Programs*, Second Edition, Berrett-Koehler Publishers (San Francisco, 2005).

Other References Which May Be Useful for various reasons
(including some popular basic textbooks on management and statistics)

Adams, Scott. *Dogbert's Top Secret Management Handbook*, Harper Collins Business Publishers (New York: 1997).

Anupindi, Ravi. *Managing Business Process Flows: Principles of Operations Management.* Prentice Hall (Englewood Cliffs NJ, 2006).

Bazerman, Max H. *Judgment in Managerial Decision Making,* Third Edition, John Wiley & Sons (New York, 1994).

Bellman, Goeffrey M. *Getting Things Done When You Are Not In Charge.* Berrett-Koehler Publishers (San Francisco, 2001).

Burrow, James L., Brad Kleindl, and Kenneth E. Everard. *Business Principles and Management.* Southwestern Educational Publishers (Cincinnati, 2007).

Goleman, Daniel, Paul Kaufman and Michael Ray, *The Creative Spirit,* Dutton (New York, 1992).

Groebner, David F., Patrick W. Shannon, Phillip C. Fry, and Kent D. Smith. *Business Statistics: A Decision-Making Approach with Student CD (6th Edition)* Prentice Hall (Englewood Cliffs NJ, 2003).

Hammer, Michael and James Champy, *Reengineering the Corporation: A Manifesto for Business Revolution,* HarperCollins (New York, 1993).

Holman, Peggy and Tom Devane, editors, *The Change Handbook: Group Methods for Changing the Future.* Berrett-Koehler Publishers (San Francisco, 1999).

Jacobs, Robert W. *Real time Strategic Change.* Berrett-Koehler Publishers (San Francisco, 1997).

Kemp, Steven M, Sid Kemp, and Steven Kemp. *Business Statistics Demystified.* McGraw-Hill Professional (New York, 2004)

Kirkpatrick, Donald L. *Developing Supervisors and Team Leaders (Improving Human Performance)* Butterworth-Heinemann (Woburn MA, 2001)

Koontz, Harold, and Heinz Weihrich, *Management: A Global Perspective.* Eleventh Edition, McGraw-Hill (New York, 2004).

Levine, David M., Timothy C. Krehbiel, and Mark L. Berenson. *Business Statistics: First Course and Student CD (4th Edition).* Prentice-Hall (Englewood Cliffs NJ, 2005).

McKnight, Wil and Elwood Chapman. *The New Supervisor: Stepping up with Confidence (A Crisp Fifty-Minute Book).* Crisp Learning (Mississauga, Ontario, 2002).

McLagan, Pat. *Change is Everybody's Business.* Berrett-Koehler Publishers (San Francisco, 2002).

Mitroff, Ian. *Smart Thinking for Crazy Times.* Berrett-Koehler Publishers (San Francisco, 1998).

Nicholas, John M. *Project Management for Business and Engineering, Second Edition: Principles and Practice.* Butterworth-Heinemann (Woburn MA, 2004)

Robinson, Alan G. and Sam Stern. *Corporate Creativity: How Innovation and Improvement Really Happen.* Berrett-Koehler Publishers (San Francisco, 1998).

Rowe, Alan J. and James D. Boulgarides, *Managerial Decision Making,* Macmillan (New York, 1992).

Rue, Leslie W. and Lloyd L. Byars. *Supervision: Key Link to Productivity*. McGraw Hill - Irwin (New York, 2003).

Shtub, Avraham, Jonathan F. Bard and Shlomo Globerson, *Project Management: Engineering, Technology, and Implementation*, Prentice-Hall (Englewood Cliffs, NJ, 1994).

Srikanth, Mokshagundam L. and Scott A. Robertson, *Measurements for Effective Decision Making: A Guide for Manufacturing Companies*, Spectrum Publishing (Guilford, CT, 1995).

Taylor, Frederick Winslow. *The Principles of Scientific Management*. Kessinger Publishing (Whitefish MT, 2006).

Weiss, W.H., *Decision Making for First Time Managers*, Amacom (New York, 1985).

Contents and use of the computer support disk

The computer disk supplied with this book includes a variety of supplemental support materials. It should automatically start up when inserted in your computer. On this disk you will find:

- Basic pre and post test on the subjects of decision making and problem solving.
- Printable Decision Data Forms that tie in with Chapter Three
  - Decision Analysis Sheet
  - Information Collection Sheet
  - Finalizing the Decision Sheet
- Templates for many of the tools discussed in the book
- Hyperlinks to selected websites
- Answers to some chapter questions & exercises plus key points of each chapter.
- A printable format for proposal development which ties in with Chapter Seven
- And other things, including additional examples of some of the tools.

Subsequent printings of this book may include updated materials on the computer support disk.

Index

About the Author

Photo courtesy of
www.ericvaughnphotography.

Robert H. Vaughn, Ph.D., RODP, is president of Arvon Management Services, the former Dean of Business and Professor Emeritus of Management at Lakeland Community College near Cleveland, Ohio. His background includes management and staff positions in the fields of publishing, training, banking, industrial engineering, human resources planning, the military and higher education.

He holds undergraduate degrees in industrial management and journalism, an MBA in OB/OD, a Ph.D. in Business Administration, and has additional postgraduate coursework in adult education. He has had articles published in a variety of professional journals and been a speaker at several regional and national conferences. He is listed in Who's Who ® in American Business and Industry.

Bob is also the author of *The Professional Trainer: A Comprehensive Guide to Planning, Delivering and Evaluating Training Programs* (2005), published by Berrett-Koehler.

You can contact Bob with comments or suggestions through his web site: www.ArvonManagement.com.